STEPS AND STAGES: FROM 9 TO 12

The Preteen Years

STEPS AND STAGES: FROM 9 TO 12

The Preteen Years

Holly Bennett and Teresa Pitman

KEY PORTER BOOKS

Canadian Cataloguing in Publication Data

Pitman, Teresa
    Steps & stages 9-12: the preteen years

(Steps & stages guides)
ISBN 1-55013-976-2

1. Preteens. 2. Child development. 3. Child rearing. I. Bennett, Holly, 1957- .
II. Title. III. Title: steps and stages nine to twelve. IV. Series: Pitman, Teresa. Steps & stages guides.

HQ777.15.P57   1998   649'.124   C97-932794-6

The publisher gratefully acknowledges the support of the Canada Council for the Arts and the Ontario Arts Council for its publishing program.

THE CANADA COUNCIL | LE CONSEIL DES ARTS
FOR THE ARTS | DU CANADA
SINCE 1957 | DEPUIS 1957

Key Porter Books Limited
70 The Esplanade
Toronto, Ontario
Canada M5E 1R2

www.keyporter.com

Electronic Formatting: Jean Lightfoot Peters

Printed and bound in Canada

98 99 00 01 6 5 4 3 2 1

Contents

Acknowledgements

AS ALWAYS, OUR THANKS MUST GO FIRST TO THE PARENTS and professionals who have been so generous with their time, thoughtful about our questions, and honest in sharing their experiences with children.

To Bonny Reichert and our other editors, past and present, at *Today's Parent*, and to our Key Porter editor Barbara Berson, who handled the sticky business of editing an editor with grace and helped us turn a motley collection of columns into a series of real books.

To Holly's husband, John Hoffman—an inspiring father, ever-supportive partner, and all-round Renaissance guy.

And last, but not least, to the kids—ours and everyone else's—who help us grow as parents and as people.

First Words

ONE OF THE MOST STRIKING THINGS ABOUT PRETEENS is how different they all are. Chances are your nine-year-old is still very much a kid, more interested in having fun than in being cool. Three years later, she'll be a self-conscious almost-teen, probably working hard to distance herself from childhood.

But preteens of the same age are very different from each other, too. Look at any group of 12-year-olds, and you'll notice that some of them have gone through puberty while others still have children's bodies. Some have reached their full adult height, while others have a foot or more of growing still to do. And those obvious physical differences are matched by varying levels of emotional maturity and by interests that range from playing with dolls to dating.

While books about babies can tell you when to expect your child to roll over, sit up, and take his first steps, the developmental sequence is not so predictable in the preteen years. Despite their differences, though, 9- to 12-year-olds do have a lot in common as well. They've moved beyond their home into the wider world, mastered the skills of childhood, and started to peek around the next corner to check out adolescence.

Whether you're dealing with a moody child coping with the changes of puberty, a music video addict, or a sometimes charming, sometimes impossible kid who picks on her little brother, it can help to know that other families have faced these challenges, too.

Wherever your preteen is on the road to adolescence and adulthood, we hope you'll find him or her in these pages. And we hope you'll find ideas about how to keep in touch with each other, to sort out conflicts, and to enjoy the new directions your relationship is taking.

Holly Bennett   *Teresa Pitman*

FREEDOM AND RESPONSIBILITY
Growing Pains and Pleasures

THESE ARE YEARS OF GROWING COMPETENCE—and confidence. Your preteen is likely enjoying a heady sense of independence that, unlike that of a toddler, is based on reality: He can ride his bike to school, spend his own money at the mall, send an e-mail to an out-of-town friend, and make himself a grilled-cheese sandwich. At the same time, you may notice bemusing pockets of dependence: Maybe

1

he still wants you to help him run the hot water for his shower, or tell the hair stylist what kind of cut he wants. That's okay. Kids not only mature at different rates from each other, but each individual child will mature more quickly in some areas and less quickly in others.

In many ways, these are "the golden years": Your child is big enough not to require the constant supervision and care that a younger child needs, but isn't yet pushing too hard for the freedoms teenagers yearn for. But the signs of the approaching teen years are there, and parents sometimes panic a little as they realize that high school, dating, and (omigod!) driving are around the corner. Will she be prepared to handle these challenges? There's no need to panic— but this *is* a good time to take stock, and to look for ways to allow your child to practise handling more decisions and responsibilities on her own.

ONE RULE, TWO RULES, OLD RULES, NEW RULES: YOUR FAMILY'S "HOUSE RULES"

Why can't I eat ice cream on the living-room couch? *You* eat on the couch!" Ouch. It's true. The "no eating in the living room" rule made sense when your kids were preschoolers, and really were more likely to dribble and spill than the adults. But a ten-year-old?

As children get older, it naturally makes sense to re-evaluate your family rules and routines to make sure they are still appropriate. Old rules need to be relaxed in acknowledgement of children's increasing independence and competence; new rules may be needed to cover situations like staying home alone. But growing up is a gradual process that tends to sneak up on us; busy as we are with the millions of details of daily life, we don't always recognize when our old way of doing things has become obsolete.

Don't worry. Your children—especially the almost-teenage ones—will be sure to notify you. Emphatically.

"Developmentally, preteens are beginning to understand the reasons behind the rules—that these aren't just arbitrary edicts from on high, but conventions that help a group of people co-operate and live comfortably together," observes Diane Prato, a London, Ontario, counsellor and author of *Let's Talk about Parenting* and *Living with Teens*. "At the same time, they are beginning to challenge and question things—including their parents and family—in a more sophisticated way. And they push against the rules as part of their push towards more independence."

Prato recommends including older children in discussions of what the rules will be and giving them input into what are reasonable limits and

3

THE HAZARDS OF HOUSEWORK

Until now, your child's household chores may have been mainly token contributions. Now, though, children are capable of handling bigger jobs, and many parents are more than ready for some significant help around the house. From now on, chores are likely to be a subject of frequent (and heated) discussion.

How much preteens are expected to do varies widely, from almost nothing to a daunting list of daily and weekly chores. Most experts advise aiming for middle ground—enough work to make a real contribution and to establish the principle that everyone in the family has some responsibility for "maintenance," but not so much that it interferes with homework, after-school activities, or adequate play time (yes, play is still very important for these kids).

There will be resistance, of course. Why should he pick up someone else's old newspapers? The compost is disgusting and he's *never* going to touch it! Most parents find they have better co-operation if they are willing to negotiate, rather than simply assign, chores. The family meeting works well for this, since everyone's chores have to add up to a workable household system. Some possible points of discussion:

- **WHICH CHORES?** If she dislikes washing dishes, but doesn't mind laundry, why not? Be flexible, but defend your own interests, too: if spray-cleaning the bathroom mirrors is not as valuable to you as dishwashing, then it's not a fair trade.
- **WHEN DO THEY NEED TO BE DONE?** Does your child hate starting his weekend with your Saturday morning clean-up? When would he prefer to do his chores? If he can make a firm commitment that meets your needs, maybe you could live with a different routine.

expectations. "In some families, the family meeting can be a good way of doing this," says Prato (see "Working It Out Together," page 33). "It's a nice way to build in the kids' input and find solutions to a conflict or problem." Other families find they can accomplish the same thing informally, around the dinner table or simply as issues arise.

At the same time (and despite their brave talk), these kids are not

- **WHAT KIND OF SYSTEM?** Do you have a fairly structured system (everyone's list on the fridge, to be checked off when completed), or do you prefer to be more informal (everyone picks up their own stuff, and kids help out when asked)? What would the kids prefer? Do they want assigned chores that they stick with for a while, or would they like the novelty of switching the chores around each week? Do you need some system for rotating the most hated chore?
- **WHAT STANDARDS?** Show your child how to do the chore in question, and try for agreement on standards. Be realistic—you are not going to get a "Molly Maid" shine from an 11-year-old boy, but you *can* expect a decently clean bathroom sink.

Finally, as kids get older it's useful to give them an area of responsibility (their own laundry, for example), that they can be in charge of. This helps them learn to be aware of what needs to be done and to plan ahead (will my favourite shirt be clean for the party Saturday?), rather than just follow your instructions.

grown-ups yet. They still need their parents to be the leaders of the family. "Sometimes you just have to hold firm," says Prato. When a rule is important, either from a health, safety, or ethical viewpoint, most parents are comfortable saying no. But Prato says it's also OK to have some rules simply because you, the parent, need them for your own well-being. "A child, for example, may think she should be able to stay up until midnight—and she may, in fact, be able to handle that just fine. But if the parents feel they really need an hour of 'downtime' at the end of the day, that's reasonable. They may be able to negotiate a compromise—for example, that the child should be ready for bed and in her room on school nights by ten, but can read or listen to the radio, and can stay up later on weekends."

What kind of rules do you need? That depends a lot on your family's style, and on the temperament and maturity of your kids. Some children need more structure, for longer, than others—for them, explicit rules may be important well into their teens. Your family circumstances make a difference, too—you can bet that a family of four kids will have more rules about fighting, sharing, and other interpersonal conflicts than a family with a single child!

When asked about the rules for her two boys (nine and twelve), Susan Newman is hard put to think of any. "There is an underlying theme or expectation of mutual respect. But you know, we really don't have that many specific rules.

"It's not a free-for-all around here or anything," Susan hastens to add. "I do nail the boys for inappropriate behaviour, but we tend to talk about it in terms of the need to be responsible, or considerate, or ethical—not in terms of rule-breaking. I would expect them, for example, to hang up their jackets rather than leave them in a heap on the kitchen floor—but I wouldn't say, 'The rule is, you have to hang up your jacket.' It's a broader principle: Everybody should look after their own stuff, so other people don't have to."

Susan acknowledges that this approach has worked well for them partly because her boys tend to be "easy" kids. "We don't have rigorous rules about when homework needs to be done or about food or bedtime, because these things haven't been a problem," she says. "If one of the boys wasn't doing well at school, or was eating a lot of junk food instead of dinner, then we might do things differently."

Susan also finds that more and more, as her kids get older, the family rules they do have are just that—expectations that apply to *everyone* in the family. "For example, we all let each other know where we are when we're not at home. I need that from the kids so I know they're safe, but Rob (my husband) and I do the same. I don't allow eating around the computer, but that goes for everyone."

For many years to come, there will also be situations, of course, where the rules for the adults *are* different than those for the kids. As Prato points out, "being fair does not necessarily mean being exactly equal." Different siblings may also have different limits, privileges, and responsibilities, depending on their ages, and that can be completely appropriate, despite their impassioned protests ("It's not fair! Alyssa got to watch *Scream*, so I should get to see a restricted movie, too!").

But whether your rules are many or few, as kids near the teen years, it's important to start talking to them about the principles and values behind your family's way of doing things, as Susan and Rob have done. After all, it's these principles—not the rules themselves—that will guide them as they make their way in the world.

STEPPIN' OUT: INTO THE WORLD—
WITHOUT YOU

an Josh and I take the bus down to the mall?" "I don't want you to come swimming with us. Just drop us off at the pool, OK?" "I want to ride my bike to the video store by myself and rent a movie."

Here it is: a rite of passage disguised in a casual question. The signal that from now on, your child will be working to throw off that cloak of parental protection you've so lovingly wrapped around her, so as to try her own wings. Freedom calls. Are you ready? Is she?

Many Canadian nine-year-olds have hardly spent an unsupervised moment. Some have never even walked to school by themselves. Yet these same kids, by 12, may be quite independent: transporting themselves, by bus or on foot, at least part of the time; enjoying movies, sports events, or "walking around downtown" with their friends; perhaps babysitting other kids. How do they achieve this transformation? It's a disconcerting question for many parents.

"One of our first issues was movies," says Deborah St. Lawrence, whose oldest daughter, Mackenzie, has just turned 13. "By 10 or 11 she wanted to be dropped off at the mall, rather than going with me. So we set some guidelines. She had to be with a group of friends, and at first I'd wait to make sure they got in and be waiting outside the ticket booth when the movie was over. Now I'll just drop them outside the mall. Of course now she wants to take a bus to the mall, and shop as well as see a movie, so there are new negotiations around that!"

Mary Gordon, administrator of parenting programs with the Toronto Board of Education, encourages parents to negotiate rules with their children, to listen and help them articulate their arguments. After all, if we didn't allow our children to push back our limits bit by bit, we might never let go. Besides, argues Gordon, "Children who understand your reasoning, and can express their own, are better prepared to withstand peer pressure." So when you're not sure about your child's request, you might take up parent educator Barbara Coloroso's suggestion and say, "Here are my concerns. Convince me."

At the same time, parents shouldn't be afraid to say, "No," or "Not this year," says Gordon. "Most children still don't have good judgement at this age," she explains, "so parents have to be prepared to keep the final responsibility, to make decisions that are in the child's best interest even if it means being unpopular."

How can we increase the odds that our children's first adventures without us will be safe and successful?

First, it's important to accommodate your child's individual make-up. Mother of four Barb Hilts notes that although her two older children (Jamie, 13, and Katherine, 12) are close in age, they have very different personalities: "Katherine is more cautious, and would be reluctant, for example, to go to the store alone on her bike, whereas Jamie really enjoys biking to his friend's or to the store for me." Children in this age range may be at quite different stages of development, notes Gordon, so your child may not be ready for an adventure his friend—or sibling—handles with ease.

Second, preparation and some basic ground rules build a safety net that will make you both feel more secure (even though your child may not admit it):

Ground rules. The bottom line, says Gordon, is that the parent "always knows where the child is and who she's with." Other sensible precautions: kids walk or go places with friends, not alone; parties must be supervised by an adult; kids always have money for a phone call (or, if appropriate, a cab).

Some rules may not be permanent, but allow peace of mind when a child takes a new step. "Call when you get there" is a time-honoured parental demand. When Mackenzie started riding the Toronto subway

SHOPLIFTING

Do children this young really shoplift? Once they start going to stores on their own or with friends, the temptation is definitely there, and not just for kids who are genuinely short of money, either. Shoplifting is as much about bravado and risk-taking as about really wanting the object in question, and when kids are caught shoplifting it's usually for small stuff like gum or lipstick.

Constable Gary Takacs, an officer in the community services division of the Peterborough (Ontario) police force, visits grade-six classes throughout the city delivering a program called VIP (values, influences, and peers). When he talks to kids about shoplifting, Takacs stresses: "If you're part of a group and somebody steals something, you're guilty as well. On the other hand, peer pressure can be positive if somebody speaks up and says, 'Hey, put that back.'"

When Shannon McCue learned that one of her son's friends had been caught stealing a chocolate bar, she called her son Chris into the living room for a talk. "I talked with him about what he should do if any of his friends shoplift when he's with them. I said, 'I am sure that on your own you would never steal. But sometime in the next few years, it will probably happen that someone you are with *will* steal. And there may be a lot of pressure for you to join in—but don't! If someone is going to steal something, and you can't dissuade him, then don't go in the store. Make an excuse and come home. Because if you're in there with him, then you are part of it.'"

Takacs believes that encouraging preteens to think ahead about some of these tough choices is important, because kids often shoplift impulsively, without really thinking about the potential consequences—at least not until they get caught.

"Typically a security officer will apprehend the shoplifter and make a citizen's arrest. The parents will be called and the police may come as well," explains Takacs. If the police are called in, they are not likely to treat the matter lightly, because "they want to stress to the child that it's a serious offence. Children over 12 may also be charged as young offenders."

While the police may emphasize to the child the legal ramifications of her actions, parents should definitely discuss the ethical issues, suggest

Michael Schulman and Eva Mekler, authors of *Bringing Up a Moral Child*. Point out how the store owners end up paying for every item stolen. Point out how stealing may make retailers hesitate to welcome kids into their stores, and hurts the community by building a climate of distrust and suspicion. An effective consequence, they suggest, would be some type of volunteer activity that allows the child to give back something positive to the community.

Discovering that your child has been involved in shoplifting is not easy. It shakes your trust in your child at a time when he is seeking (and needs) more independence. (And it may be an appropriate consequence to allow him only supervised access to stores for a period of time.) But there's no need to foresee a lifetime of delinquency and dishonesty. The reality is, quite a few preteens and teens try shoplifting at least once—on a dare, for a thrill, or in an unthinking moment of greed. It's a serious mistake, but handled well, it's also a valuable learning opportunity.

to visit her dad, Deborah St. Lawrence stipulated that she travel during rush hour (safety in numbers), and with a friend.

Streetproofing. This, says Gordon, is not a "single two-hour lecture" but an ongoing discussion of safety issues as they arise in everyday life. For example, if a child is walking to a friend's house alone for the first time, it makes sense to discuss the best route (and routes to avoid), and where the child could get help if needed (i.e., "If anyone bothers you, you could run in that corner store and tell the clerk"). It's also important to review basic safety rules. Says Deborah: "Mackenzie has to walk by a long strip where it's a cemetery on both sides of the road, on her way to school. People have stopped to ask her directions there. I remind her that adults should know better than to ask a child, and that she should never stop or go near their car."

Gordon stresses that the goal of streetproofing is not to scare the wits out of a child, but to equip her to handle herself. "Our own insecurities can erode their confidence," she says. "We can't give in to the fear of letting them go."

"Friendproofing." As every parent knows too well, friends aren't always a good influence. Gordon urges parents to teach and rehearse "refusal skills" with their kids. "Help your child come up with something to say that sounds strong—like 'No, I'm expected home now,'—not apologetic or weak," she says. Peer-pressure issues heat up in the teen years, so it's a good idea to start talking about them now, when the stakes aren't so high.

Practice runs. An easily overlooked way of preparing our children to start leaving the nest is to give them plenty of opportunities to master worldly skills while they're with us. When we go places with our kids, we tend to navigate, pay, and order for them. Yet by inviting them to order the pizza, figure out which bus route to take, or buy the milk while we wait in the car, we help them develop "a sense of knowing how to conduct themselves in the world," says Gordon. That just might make the difference between a child who can ask for help and a child who is too shy to speak up; or between a child who has the self-confidence to head home when his friends get out of hand and one who goes along because he can't figure out what else to do.

"Parents should be constantly on the lookout for new opportunities for independence and confidence-building," says Gordon. Stepping out into the world does involve a degree of risk. But with your guidance, the risks will be manageable and your child well-prepared. Then you can admire and applaud—rather than fear—your child's newfound independence.

HOME ALONE: BYE, BYE BABYSITTER!

t nine, Daniel is clearly too young to stay at home alone. His sister Sarah, who is 12, is quite comfortable on her own, and even babysits for other families on occasion. That's quite a transition to make in just three short years.

Helping your child make that transition can require some long-range planning, according to Wendy Shusterman, the mother of Sarah, twelve, and Daniel, nine. "By the time Sarah was ten, we could see this coming. She was getting bored of staying with her babysitter after school, and wanting to take on more responsibility," says Wendy.

Sarah had given her parents some pretty clear indications that she was ready to stay at home alone. But before her first "trial run," there was some groundwork to be laid.

Wendy's first step to prepare the kids for staying on their own (not for everyone, though) was to buy a dog. "I felt the dog would give Sarah and Daniel a greater feeling of security, knowing the dog would bark if a stranger came around to the house. The dog also gives them a sense of responsibility—they are the ones who take care of him."

Wendy has a car phone, and both children have memorized that number. "It really helps that they can contact me so easily. When I'm at work, I always tell people where I'm going so I can be tracked down quickly if one of the kids calls." Her availability is reassuring to all of them.

But Wendy also began setting up a support network of friends and neighbours. It's important for kids alone to have access to immediate help. The phone numbers of the family across the street and other friends close by are posted near the Shustermans' phone. Wendy remembers that "some of my friends offered to be a back-up for me and I've taken them up on it—it reduces the stress knowing that the kids can call them if they need to."

WHO YA GONNA CALL? WHAT A HOME-ALONE KID SHOULD KNOW
- **Where you are and how to reach you; who to call instead if you are unavailable**
- **A nearby neighbour she can go to when immediate help is needed (there's a fire or she hurt herself)**
- **911 number (if your community has it) and other emergency phone numbers, and when to use them**
- **Where the fire extinguisher is, how to use it, and when to stop trying and get out of the house**
- **What to do if someone comes to the door; what to say if someone phones (should he answer? Should he say you're not there, or that you can't come to the phone?)**
- **Where the Band-Aids and other essential first-aid stuff are**
- **What she's *not* allowed to use (oven, fireplace, tools?) or do (leave the house, have friends over?)**

Wendy's final preparatory step was to define the "home alone rules." That, she found, required some balancing. She didn't want to scare Sarah and Daniel by listing every possible emergency, but she wanted to be sure they felt prepared.

It's most helpful to give children some specific guidelines about safety routines (see "Who Ya Gonna Call?" above). These might include making sure the door is locked, not answering the door if someone knocks, letting the answering machine screen phone calls, using the toaster but not the stove, etc.

Then you can play "what if?" and let the child suggest her own solutions. What if you dropped a glass on the floor and it broke? What if you came home from school and the front door was open? What if there was a storm and the power went off? Listen not just to your child's answers, but to how she feels about being alone in that situation—if the answers make sense but the child is clearly nervous or apprehensive, it might be better to wait.

Your back-up list of adults to call is crucial here, too. Kids should not feel as though they have to cope with emergencies, or even more minor problems, on their own. Emphasize that whenever they're concerned, afraid, or don't know what to do, they should call someone.

The Shustermans tested things out by starting with short trips to the store and to visit friends in the neighbourhood, then gradually extended the length of time that Sarah was left at home. So far, it's worked out fine—even when the kids have run into the unexpected.

Wendy recalls two situations when Sarah was confronted with a problem she wasn't sure how to handle. Once last summer, Sarah's neighbourhood day camp got out unexpectedly early. She normally walked home with her little brother (who attended a different group), and now she didn't know what to do. The idea of waiting for him alone on the street corner made her nervous, but if she just went home by herself, he wouldn't know where she was. So she went to the nearby home of her former sitter, had a drink, and called her mother for further instructions.

On another occasion, Sarah and Daniel had come home from school and actually gone into the house when they thought they smelled gas. Sarah quickly called a neighbour, and the children headed over to the neighbour's house.

"It turned out to be a false alarm," Wendy says, "but I was very pleased by the way she handled both situations. You can teach your children how to handle various problems or emergencies, but they still need access to an adult in case something comes up."

How can you tell if *your* child is ready to stay home alone? It depends on both your child and the situation. John Tee, supervisor with the Halton (Ontario) Children's Aid Society, explains that the law in this

RECOMMENDED READING

Alone at Home: A Kid's Guide, by Ann Banks, Puffin Books, 1989.

Home Alone Kids: The Working Parent's Complete Guide, by Bryan Robinson, Bobbie Rowland, and Mick Coleman, Lexington Books, 1989.

area is deliberately vague, relying on terms such as "adequate supervision" to define when a child can safely and legally be left alone, because there are no hard and fast rules.

What's important is that besides actually being safe, he also *feels* safe. The imaginative or nervous child might need an adult's comforting presence longer than the sceptical child who laughs at scary shows on TV. If you don't know your neighbours well enough for your child to turn to them in an emergency, it would probably be better to arrange for a sitter. Younger siblings, too, complicate the situation (see our next chapter!), and can either provide reassuring company or add more stress and responsibility than a child can handle.

Like Wendy Shusterman, Tee stresses the importance of slowly and gradually preparing your child for being left on his own. "Start with just ten or fifteen minutes," he says.

A final note: Even after your child is quite comfortable home alone, be aware of his limits. There can be a vast difference in a child's comfort level between, for example, a couple of hours after school and a long, late-night stretch. Wendy observes, "I've met parents who seem to think that once their children can manage alone for an hour or two, then it's OK to leave them alone all day, every day—say, during the summer while they're at work. I think that's too hard on the kids. They might cope, but they feel stressed and lonely."

As in so many other aspects of parenting, the real key here is knowing your child and what he is ready for.

MY BROTHER'S KEEPER: BABYSITTING YOUNGER SIBLINGS

he first time 12-year-old Jason babysat his two younger brothers, his parents were on pins and needles. "We weren't sure it would work out," recalls Jason's dad, Jim Barton. "Jason can be quite an excitable kid, and the three boys together are sometimes a handful for adults! But he really wanted to do it, and his brothers (nine and five) liked the idea. So we went out for lunch, and hurried back an hour later."

Almost a year later, Jason's parents now leave him "in charge" confidently. "It's funny," muses Jim. "The boys often have a lot of conflict. But they clearly act differently when they're on their own. They make it work. Jason knows his job is to be a 'sitter,' not a 'brother,' and he takes the responsibility seriously. We've never come home to tears and complaints."

Jason's enthusiastic attitude toward looking after his brothers is one indicator of a good prospective sitter. Veronica McNeilly, director of community and volunteer development at St. John Ambulance, Oakville (Ontario) branch, says that her organization's babysitting courses describe several other qualities that parents should look for in a sitter.

"The babysitter—whether it is your child or another child—needs to have plenty of energy, be flexible, understand the needs and behaviours of younger children, and have the knowledge and information to deal with problems and emergencies," McNeilly explains.

She advises parents to watch how the children get along on a day-to-day basis. Of course the dynamic can be different (for better or worse) in the parents' absence, but if you are constantly intervening in fights or arguments, then letting your older child babysit might not be a good idea. It is also more difficult to have one child "in charge" when the siblings are close in age—an 11-year-old is unlikely to be impressed by having a 12-year-old looking after her.

In the St. John Ambulance babysitting course, the instructors use role-playing to help kids learn how to handle different situations—an idea parents can adapt for use at home. Pretend to be the child who refuses to go to bed when it's bedtime, and see how your child responds. Make believe that the power has suddenly gone out during a storm, and ask what your potential babysitter would do. His reactions to these role-playing situations will help you determine if he has the maturity and knowledge to take care of his siblings.

You may want to go one step further and have your aspiring babysitter enrol in a babysitting course.

The St. John Ambulance course is geared to children 11 to 14. It teaches basic tips for such problems as crying, children who won't go to bed, and fighting. The course also covers safety guidelines, basic first-aid techniques, and information on handling emergencies. "The most important thing a babysitting class does is give the child confidence," adds McNeilly. Available across Canada, the course lasts about six and a half hours (which can be taken all at once or broken up over a number of weeks), and costs about $30. Check your phone book for the nearest branch.

Carolann Malenfant's 12-year-old daughter Sarah has recently begun babysitting her three younger brothers. Carolann says her daughter found the St. John course helpful, but she says the real secret to their successful babysitting arrangement is planning the evening. "I sit down with Sarah and the others before we go out and I plan what they'll do while we're away. Often we rent a movie for the kids so I'll say they should start the movie at seven, and tell them what snacks they can have, and then we'll put out a game or something for them to play when the movie is over."

What Carolann is doing during this planning session is showing that Sarah is in the position of authority in her absence. So when Sarah says, "OK, it's seven o'clock, time to start the movie," the others know that it isn't just her idea.

BABYSITTING SIBLINGS: THE HORROR STORY

Just in case it all sounds too rosy, and you're wondering why *your* kids don't get along like that, here's a true confession from Holly's childhood:

"When we were way too old for babysitters, my poor parents still had to hire them because my younger brother and I fought so viciously. Every once in a while they'd try to leave us, but it often backfired. The worst incident occurred when I was 13. My ten-year-old brother was being, in my eyes, so awful that I decided I had to call my parents. But every time I went to dial he would cut the connection. I was running frantically between the kitchen phone and the bedroom extension, trying to make the call. Finally, in desperation, I whacked him—hard—on the head with the telephone receiver. He went ballistic, totally enraged. I ran out of the house in tears to my friend's house across the street, to ask to use *her* phone. The door was answered by her 16-year-old brother... who had just shaved his head. Is there anything more mortifying than blubbering in front of an older boy with no hair? I don't think so."

There *is* an encouraging ending to this story: "My brother and I are really good friends now. We like each other, and neither of us is prone to violent rages. But it must have been a long wait for our parents!"

Jim also mentions this as an important part of preparing for sibling babysitters: "You have to support the one who is babysitting by going over the ground rules publicly, but you also have to make sure the older sibling doesn't abuse his authority. We don't set Jason up to be a disciplinarian, or make a big deal about things like bedtime. His job is primarily to make sure everyone is safe and help the younger boys have a nice time."

Clearly, having a sibling babysit is convenient for parents—no driving a sitter home afterwards, no need for detailed instructions about household routines and where things are. But are there disadvantages to this arrangement?

Leslie Hennin, mother of 12-year-old Melissa, who often babysits her three younger siblings, feels that fighting between the kids is the big issue. "It's very hard for the older child to enforce discipline," says Leslie. "My solution has been to tell the one who's babysitting to write down any problems she has with the younger children, and then I'll deal with it when we get home." Carolann agrees: "The children have to be receptive to this arrangement. If I had a child who was a real behaviour problem, or the older child didn't get along with a younger child, I'd hire a babysitter instead. It only works if they want to do it."

Parents sometimes wrestle with the question of whether or not the babysitting sibling should be paid.

Carolann is very clear: "I never pay them to babysit. I think they should do it out of the kindness of their hearts, as part of being in the family. I do make an effort to rent a movie, or buy chips and pop, so that it is a treat for all of them."

Leslie, however, has taken a different approach. "If we're going out for dinner or an evening, I pay Melissa the same as I would pay another babysitter. After all, she may have given up another babysitting job to help us out. But often she watches the kids while I run out to pick up a few groceries or go to the bank, and I don't pay her on those occasions." The Bartons have a similar arrangement with Jason.

Overall, babysitting in the family can be convenient for parents and beneficial for the young babysitter. "They love the chance to be in charge," Leslie says, "and I think it gives them more confidence when they go out to babysit other kids. Melissa is often asked to babysit, partly because people know she's had the experience of caring for younger children at home."

"I think this is good for Jason as well as us," adds Jim. "I can see that he feels good that we trust him to handle things well."

All agree that older siblings shouldn't be asked to babysit too much, as this can create resentment. But with proper preparation and support, babysitting younger siblings can be a valuable learning experience for the oldest child, and a good bonding experience for all siblings.

"I WANT WAGES!" EARNING MONEY

his is a hard age when it comes to money," complains ten-year-old Catherine Harrison. "You want more things than little kids do, but you're too young for a real job." Is earning their own money a good idea for preteens? Some parents say no, and prefer to give their children allowances or simply give them money when they need it. But Roberta Garriock, mother of ten-year-old Matthew and eight-year-old Andrew, says: "I found that when Matt started working for his money, he really began to understand its value. He's not so quick to spend on something junky because he knows what it took to earn those dollars."

Preteens today may have a harder time finding work than in the past. Take the traditional paper route, for example, that financed many kids a generation ago. Now many papers are delivered by adults before the sun rises; when kids do have paper routes parents often feel nervous about allowing them to go out to collect payment from door to door.

"I had a paper route where I had to collect, and it was a problem," says 12-year-old Noah Hicks. "People wouldn't be home, and I'd have to keep going back to get the money, or I wouldn't have enough change for them. Now I have a straight delivery route, no collecting. I don't make as much money, but it's much easier."

Noah shows his entrepreneurial style by taking any papers he has left over from his route and selling them to neighbours who don't subscribe. "I almost always get a few extra, and they expect you to just throw them away."

His other main money-making effort is pretty traditional—babysitting a five-year-old who lives nearby.

Noah says he gets a lot out of what he does. "I really like working and feeling useful. People appreciate it when I bring them their papers,

EARNING MONEY: FINDING A BALANCE

We all admire kids who get out there and earn their own money: They're showing responsibility, commitment, a readiness to work hard, all kinds of good qualities. But some parents worry that too much early "money-making" (which often grows into regular part-time work in high school), can eat into kids' school and play time.

Take Karl. At 12, he has a daily paper route, plus a job on weekends helping to set up and tear down a flea market. He likes the money he earns, and the stuff he can buy with it. But he's had to stop playing hockey this year, because too many games conflicted with his weekend work, and he can't participate in any after-school activities either because he has to deliver papers.

Earning a little money gives preteens a sense of accomplishment and freedom that's valuable. But that has to be balanced with the other things that are important in their lives: time with friends, time to pursue interests and hobbies, time for homework. If your child is giving up valuable activities in order to earn spending money, you might want to consider increasing his allowance or offering a more flexible way for him to earn money at home.

or when I babysit for them. And it's great having my own money that I earned myself when I want to buy something."

Sometimes, kids like Noah feel frustrated when they can't get "real" jobs because of their age. Many parents help by paying for household chores. "I won't pay for regular chores, like cleaning up her room," explains David Harrison, the father of three girls, including Catherine. "But if they want to do something big, like cleaning out the garage or sweeping up all the leaves, I'll pay them for that."

He finds, however, that this arrangement sometimes leads to conflict. "It gets frustrating when I tell Catherine she hasn't done the job well enough, and then she starts complaining about it being too hard." David concludes that this type of family friction is one of the hazards when kids work for their parents rather than for someone else.

Despite these tribulations, many parents see valuable benefits when preteens earn their own money.

Roberta Garriock, whose son Matt has a Sunday-only paper route, says, "I think it has really helped him to learn some money management skills. He started this job because we don't give him an allowance, and I think he felt like all the other kids he knew had money and he didn't. He just wanted some money of his own to spend."

Matt likes the one-day-a-week route even though he doesn't make a lot of money, because it doesn't take up too much of his time. On his own, he decided early on to put half of the money he earns in the bank and spend the other half.

According to Matt's mom, "He doesn't actually spend much of the spending portion either!" He has saved for some special things, like a baseball cap he wanted and Christmas gifts for his parents, but sometimes he discovers after saving up that he doesn't really want that video game or toy.

Not all preteens are interested in becoming junior entrepreneurs, or even in doing household chores for cash. Those who are, though, often find that earning their own cash, their own way, gives them some insight into the adult world, and a little mad money in their pockets.

"YOU'RE GROUNDED!" DOES HOUSE ARREST MAKE SENSE?

aren Sterling didn't know where her daughter was. Jennette, like many children before her, had run off to play at a friend's house without telling anybody. Karen didn't exactly panic—a couple of quick phone calls established Jennette's whereabouts—but she was understandably upset. Jennette was summoned home and grounded.

Karen uses this particular consequence more than she likes. She says it seldom works very well and it often backfires. After all, there's nothing a computer addict, like her 12-year-old son Geoff, likes more that being banned from going out. Besides, confining kids to the house means that she has to police it. "I don't have the time or energy to do that," she admits.

Parent educator Mary Gordon is well aware of these drawbacks. She believes that grounding, which she defines as the loss of outside-the-house privileges, is overused by parents.

With any consequence, Gordon says, the key question is, "Is it reasonable?" She points out that children are often grounded for things that happen inside the home, and "to deny access to friends and activities outside the home as a consequence of failing to comply with expectations inside the home is not reasonable. If they haven't done their chores because they were watching TV, grounding is not a good consequence, but it would be reasonable to say they can't watch TV until chores are done."

Gordon suggests that grounding be reserved for misbehaviour related to being outside the home. "For example, if you say, 'Be home at five,' and your child keeps wandering in at six-thirty, then grounding him the next day makes sense. He has lost the privilege of the freedom to play, for a *short time*," she says.

We also need to keep in mind what we're taking away from our children when we isolate them from their peers. Karen says, "Geoff doesn't spend nearly enough time with his friends, so to take his time with them away from him as punishment seems self-defeating." Gordon adds, "A child's job at this age is to learn to hang out. Kids who have connections with other kids do better in school, they're happier. We sometimes think this time with friends isn't productive, but it is."

So why do parents resort to grounding so frequently? "I think that sometimes it's almost an impulse," Gordon observes. "In a pinch we go back to the familiar things. Many of us were raised on 'a swat when they're little, grounded when they're big.'" Indeed, parental control often seems to be slipping away as our kids hit the preteen years, and grounding may seem like a quick way to reassert some control.

"It's almost like at this age they're saying, 'Prove you're serious,'" says Donna Della-Picca, a mother of nine- and eleven-year-old boys. She argues that, if used sparingly (she does it once or twice a year) grounding can be both appropriate and effective. "At their age, size, and intelligence, there's not much I can do. They don't care about time out or a cancelled TV program. It has to be something major before they really notice."

Donna once grounded her 11-year-old son Bryan while the family was on the way to see the Moscow circus. He had a major tantrum and swore at her. "He totally crossed the line," she says. "My husband took him home and they both missed the circus. I still feel bad about it because that circus was a once-in-a-lifetime opportunity, but his behaviour really improved for a long time after," she says.

In the long run, though, Gordon argues that grounding does little to help a child learn to self-discipline, and it can easily spiral into an unproductive power struggle. "Everybody forgets what the original issue was," she says. "Let's think in terms of encouraging good behaviour instead of punishing wrong behaviour. Give them a clear understanding of what you expect. Set up the conditions *before* the negative behaviour happens."

ALTERNATIVES TO GROUNDING

First, let's review the basics. *Before* it comes to misbehaviour and consequences, do you:

- Make your expectations clear and specific?
- Make sure your child hears and understands your expectations?
- Negotiate some rules, within reasonable limits?
- Praise or show your appreciation for responsible behaviour?

All of these are helpful steps to take in advance. Now, for those inevitable transgressions, you might consider these other options:

- **Simply remind.** Not every slip-up requires a heavy consequence! If your child is usually responsible but forgets to tell you one day when he goes to a friend's house, a reminder that you were worried and need to know where he is may be all that's necessary. If she forgets to feed the dog once, you can remind her. If she forgets frequently, you can help her find a strategy for remembering.
- **Make restitution.** Did she hurt her younger brother? Maybe she should do something nice for him (when she calms down), like taking over one of his chores or helping him build his new Lego set.
- **Logical consequences.** It's not always easy to find one, but if you can, a consequence that truly flows logically from the "crime" has a

At around the age of nine, children are learning how to handle independence, Gordon points out. "We expect them to be a lot more responsible and to remember things. But they love their friends and they get swept along in the moment—they forget sometimes. We have to train them to be responsible, to phone or be home at a certain time." The occasional grounding may be part of that but it doesn't need to be heavy-handed, like for a week, to be effective, Gordon believes. For one thing, prolonged grounding deprives the child of the chance to go out and succeed at being responsible and get good feedback for it.

But what if you've lost it, and sentenced your ten-year-old to a two-week grounding, and you don't think you'll survive having a grumpy preteen imprisoned in your house for that long? Admit you goofed.

greater impact, partly because it's hard for even a budding preteen lawyer to argue that it's unfair. Riding without a helmet? Maybe he'd better walk to school next week. Leaving piles of clothes and wet towels in the bathroom, no matter how often you remind? Looks like she's got some laundry to do. (Incidentally, a brief grounding can sometimes qualify here, for example, if a child heads off to the park with her friends without telling you.)

- Community service. "This is one 'illogical' consequence that I like, because it benefits me instead of causing me extra hassles," comments one mother. "I assign extra chores. It doesn't exactly fit the misbehaviour, but there's a kind of logic: You cause me worry or extra work, you make it up by helping me out."
- Withdrawing a non-beneficial privilege. Parent educators don't much like withdrawing privileges—this kind of punishment usually bears no relation to the actual misbehaviour and rates low on the "learning value" scale—but realistically, most parents resort to this when the chips are down. If you feel you must withdraw a privilege, try to stay away from those that really benefit the child. Take away TV/Nintendo time or a trip to the mall rather than a family skating excursion or time with his friends.

Gordon says, "You can say, 'I was really worried and I overdid it. It wasn't fair so I'm reducing the time.'"

An admission like this doesn't result in a parent losing face. In fact it has a positive payoff in the long term, Gordon says. "Fairness really appeals to children of this age. I think you can actually gain respect if you admit you made a mistake."

Kids can admit mistakes, too. Karen Sterling's brood once "grounded" themselves. "We were on the way to a movie and there was so much fighting in the car that we turned around and went home to talk about it," says Karen. "I was prepared to give in and take them, but Jennette said, 'No, there isn't enough time now. We blew it.'"

TALKING BACK TO BACKTALK:
FROM DEFIANCE TO DEBATE

'm going to Mike's house, OK?" "Not now, honey." "What? Why not?" "Because it's a school night and you haven't done your homework yet. It's too late." "That's stupid! Who cares if it's a school night! You never let me do anything! I'm going anyway!"

Of course, print cannot quite capture the volume or tone of that last volley of words. But perhaps it sounds familiar? If you have a preteen in the house, odds are you've had at least a few of these encounters—maybe plenty. And maybe worse.

But if backtalk isn't pleasant, we can console ourselves with the fact that at this age, it's entirely normal. Diane Prato is a counsellor in London, Ontario, and author of *Let's Talk about Parenting* and *Living with Teens* (Nurturing Meadow Press). She explains, "In early adolescence defiance does emerge—kind of like in the 'terrible twos.' It's part of the growth process. Preteens are beginning to assert themselves. And they don't always do it in a very comfortable or mature style!"

As parents, we need to give our preteens room to express their viewpoints, and opportunities to practise the assertiveness and problem-solving skills that will be so important to them as young adults. But we don't want to give them the idea that it's OK to verbally abuse people—especially us!

If backtalk is becoming an issue in your family, Prato suggests some "preventive" strategies for parents. They won't eliminate backtalk, but they will create a better climate for more appropriate behaviour:

Develop some family norms about how people speak to each other.
You've probably had a "no hitting" rule since day one. Now is a good time to agree as a family that "hurting with words"—name-calling, personal putdowns and insults, etc.—is not acceptable either.

Reward polite assertiveness. Let your preteen know that you *do* want to hear his feelings and ideas, but will be more open to negotiating solutions with him if he tries to express himself appropriately. Make it clear that insulting you or shouting at you will *not* change your mind, but that a reasonable counter-argument might. To our excitable 11-year-old, I sometimes say, "If you yell at me when I say no, the answer is still no. If you calm down and then talk to me about it, we might be able to work something out."

When your child does manage an acceptable protest, consider making larger-than-usual concessions—and let her know why. "Okay, you've explained to me very clearly and politely why you really want to stay up and watch that TV show. I'll let you watch it, if you get all your school stuff packed and yourself ready for bed beforehand."

Re-evaluate your family rules and routines in light of your pre-teen's growing maturity. This is a great time to acknowledge your child's need for more independence, suggests Prato, by gradually increasing her range of choices and areas of responsibility. Can she decide for herself when to turn out her light or do her homework? Can he have some say about which chores will be his and when they should be done? If you give her appropriate ways to exercise her independence, she might not feel the need to demand it so belligerently.

It will still happen sometimes, though. You ask your child to take out the recycling box, and you're met with a scathing indictment of your personal worth. Prato suggests several alternatives:

Listen. "Yikes, are you ever upset about something! What's up?" When kids are uncharacteristically snarly, says Prato, it's often in response to pressures that have built up through their day. "They let their frustration spill out at home, where it's safe. We can show them, by our willingness to listen, that they don't have to be so prickly in order to get our attention."

&$@!: SWEARING

Young people swearing and using colourful language is an issue of some debate among parents. Some are not particularly bothered by it—they use four-letter words themselves and don't feel shocked when their children pick them up too; others find it extremely offensive and feel strongly that this kind of language should not be permitted.

Because opinions about language vary so widely, Oakville, Ontario, grade-five teacher Rob Coverdale explains that even if your family is quite comfortable with swearing, your child needs to understand that others may not be. "Children have difficulty in understanding why the language they use at home naturally is unacceptable in the school setting." Like other social skills, kids need to learn when these words are appropriate and when they're not.

Like adults, kids sometimes swear out of sheer anger. As one of my own sons explains, "You get so mad about something that you're not thinking the way you would if you were calm, and the swear words just come out. You hear adults and other kids say them when they're mad too."

But kids also tend to swear "for fun," especially with their peers. Social worker Kathy Likavec, who spends a lot of time working with this age group, feels that this is quite normal. "Swearing can be fun. I remember driving with my nine-year-old daughter and a car full of kids. They were all singing along with a song and they all knew a swear word was coming up in the lyrics and could hardly wait to sing it out. It's being daring, being grown-up."

But what if your preteen's swearing seems to be getting out of hand?

Likavec's recommendation is that parents simply remind their children when they use swear words at inappropriate times (around grandparents, perhaps, or at school) but that they don't make a big deal out of it. "I wouldn't punish a child for swearing. If the child doesn't respond—if he keeps on swearing after you've spoken to him, or if the teacher calls because he's swearing constantly at school—you need to find out what the underlying problem is. Why is your child feeling so angry or hostile or desperate for attention? Don't worry so much about the swearing—look for the deeper problem."

Stick to the main issue. Backtalk can be a very effective way to divert our attention from the recycling! If there's a responsibility to be fulfilled, resist getting sidetracked into a big confrontation about language.

Be honest and assertive. "We don't want to lay a big guilt trip on kids, but it's good for them to know that we have personal feelings, too," says Prato. By all means tell them, "I don't like being talked to that way. That's not acceptable." If your child continues, you might need to add, "I'm not willing to be insulted," and leave.

After all, we hardly provide a good role model if we allow our children to treat us like doormats. Prato sums it up nicely: "Respecting children's feelings is important, but respecting yourself is essential!"

Don't take it personally. "Our first instinct is to do just that," acknowledges Prato. "But rarely is a child's backtalk intended as a personal attack. This usually does stem largely from developmental and outside pressures. And if a child does seem to be constantly hurtful and hostile, that is probably a signal of a larger problem which ought to be explored." (Obviously, a discussion like this has to be approached sensitively, at a calm, private time and possibly with the support of a family counsellor or child psychologist.)

Discuss more positive communication when things have calmed down. Minor infractions can often be corrected on the spot, with a good-natured "Excuse me?!" or "Sorry, I don't answer to that. Want to try again?" But if tempers are flaring, your child will not be receptive. Find a quieter time to talk about the importance of learning to assert himself respectfully—not just in the family, but with friends and colleagues throughout his life. Give him some examples of more acceptable and productive approaches he might use: "Dad, I hate it when all my friends get to do something and I don't! It's embarrassing!" or "What if I do extra chores to earn the money? Then can I go to the movie?"

And if all our listening, talking, and limit-setting seems to go in one ear and out the other, Prato urges us not to become discouraged. Kids this age "have a bit of a knee-jerk reaction against being corrected. They're not likely to say, 'Good point, Mom!' or 'You're right, I'll really learn from that consequence.' But they'll still respond."

WORKING IT OUT TOGETHER:
FAMILY MEETINGS

he family meeting. A time for parents and kids to plan together, work out problems together, develop family rules together. Carolyn Usher, publications director of the non-profit BC Council for the Family, and mother of two teenage boys, is a staunch believer in family meetings. "It's great training for life in a democracy," says Usher. "Kids learn to speak up for themselves, and to consider the impact of their decisions or demands on others. They learn to resolve conflict in a way that takes into account everyone's needs and feelings. They learn to accept and share responsibility." On a personal note, she adds, "It's given us a real sense of family solidarity, and that's a good feeling."

It sounds so good in theory. But what's the reality? A nagging inner voice advised me to find out before writing this article. I needed to see this in action.

As they say, there's no place like home. My older boys, at seven and eleven years old, were a perfect test case.

Usher says that family meetings can work well even with young children, but that the pay-offs for parents are most obvious when kids approach adolescence. Nine-to-twelve-year-olds tend to be more receptive to parental ideas than teens, but just as eager to voice their opinions, so this is an ideal age to get the family meeting habit established. "If you're still being the police when that enormous drive for independence hits, your home can become a battlefront," she advises. "But when decisions and rules are a shared responsibility, then everyone 'polices' them. The home becomes a much happier place to be."

Not that everything has to be shared. "You need to think through what is negotiable, and what isn't," Usher cautions, "and state that clearly."

So. As I prepare for writing this chapter, our first family meeting

ONE KID AT A TIME: WHEN IT'S NOT A FAMILY MATTER

Sometimes you need to talk something over with just one child, in a more private setting. She brings home a poor report card, and you need to figure out why and what to do about it. He doesn't seem to be spending time with his friends any more, and you wonder if there's a problem. She wants a clothing allowance, and that means planning a clothing list and budget together. But in a busy, noisy household, or with a less-than-forthcoming child, attempts at a "serious talk" can be frustrating. Some ideas:

- **Schedule a meeting.** You know you can't talk productively about that report card when you're shocked, she's defensive, and her little brother is buzzing around. "Let's both think about this for a while. After Tommy's in bed, I'd like to get together in the kitchen and try to figure out what went wrong."
- **Get out of the house.** Take him out for lunch, or a snack. It sets a more positive tone, takes you away from household distractions, and puts both of you on your best behaviour.
- **Talk in the car.** In the car, you're sitting close, but not actually looking at each other. And you can't take off ("I have to phone Emily!") the minute things get a bit uncomfortable. This seems to make it easier for many kids (and parents) to open up. A long drive at night (a dark car is even easier to talk in) is ideal.
- **Check in at bedtime.** Bedtime is not a good time to deal with a conflict. But when your child is lying, relaxed, in the dark, he may feel ready to confide a worry or problem. Just go sit on his bed for awhile, and chat quietly about everyday things. Leave lots of "space" in the conversation for him. If there's something specific you think is on his mind, ask.

agenda goes up on the fridge, scheduled for Sunday afternoon. Looking for something easy and fun as the first order of business, I jot down "Plan boys' summer programs" (it's spring as I write this). For several days, it's the sole agenda item. What next?

Family meetings to decide on swimming or computer camp are one thing; but this is also supposed to be an arena for creatively solving conflicts. So when indignant screaming pierces the air, and I finally get the two boys separated and semi-articulate, I make my move: "Well, guys, each of you is convinced that hologram card is yours. Jesse is sure he traded you for it, Ry, and you're sure you didn't. Why don't I keep it safe for now, and we'll put it on the agenda for our meeting tomorrow. If you solve the problem on your own before then, that's great, but otherwise, we'll all work together at our meeting to find a solution you both think is fair." More heated accusations and counter-accusations. "We'll work it out at our meeting. Right now it's allowance time." (A cheap ploy to distract them, I admit.)

Secretly, though, I'm a little worried. How much room for consensus is there in what boils down to a case of theft?

Usher has some tips for parents who'd like to start holding family meetings. First, run it like a real meeting—complete with agenda and minutes. That may seem a little stiff at first (and you can use more casual terms like "meeting plan" and "agreements" if you like), but the structure helps make sure that everyone has a chance for input and that there's some sense of accomplishment at the end. Besides, kids feel they are being taken seriously when their parents give their opinions adult weight—in writing.

Second, build in something positive in each meeting—especially in the early ones—that will give kids experience with shared decision-making in an enjoyable way (What movie should we rent on Saturday? What fun activity can we do on the weekend?).

Finally, don't be discouraged if the first meetings are a bit tumultuous. "It takes a while for people to learn negotiating skills," reassures Usher. "Plus, with older kids, there may be a backlog of complaints to deal with." While family members find their feet, a parent should chair the meeting: trying to keep things cool and civil, reminding kids that everyone will get a chance to speak, bringing the problem-solving back to the goal of a mutually acceptable solution. Eventually, the kids can take their turn at chairing and recording.

The Big Day arrives. I give a little pep talk on what we're trying to do. We sail through Item 1. Item 2: the hologram card. One advantage to this system is apparent already: Both boys are in a good mood rather than a blind fury. They exchange good-natured growls across the table. I summarize the problem briefly for my husband's benefit; move quickly into brainstorming solutions before the boys begin an interminable blow-by-blow. Would Jesse be willing to trade Ry another card to keep the hologram? Ry doesn't want any of Jesse's cards. Could Riley be willing to trade Jesse for the hologram? Not really, he doesn't have any more doubles. Would one of you be willing to buy the card from the other? Bingo. Riley would. Jesse demands 15 cents. Ry counters with 10, but is persuaded quite easily that 15 is fair. Unfortunately, he doesn't have 15 cents, having already spent his entire allowance. Finally, it's agreed: I will keep the card until Riley earns 15 cents to pay to Jesse.

RECOMMENDED READING

Raising Kids Who Can: Using Family Meetings to Nurture Responsible, Cooperative, Caring, and Happy Children, by Betty Lou Bettner and Amy Lew, HarperCollins, 1992.

OK, it was a minor issue. One measly superhero card. But it was settled amicably, creatively, and at a bearable decibel level. They're both happy with the outcome. It only took ten minutes. I'm impressed. In a flash of insight, I realize why it's been so hard to get my guys to work out their problems: I've been trying to get them to do it when they're too mad to think. It's like trying to negotiate a peace treaty on the front. I see how in family meeting kids get a chance to practise problem-solving skills away from the pressure of the original conflict. I think I'm sold.

YOU GOTTA HAVE FRIENDS

Your Preteen's Social Life

Allan Ibarra

PLAYING WITH FRIENDS HAS DOUBTLESS BEEN an important part of your child's life for a long time now. Over the next few years, though, you'll see some interesting changes in your child's friendships. Friendship becomes more intense, but also more demanding, as kids start to define who belongs to their friendship group—and who doesn't.

As children approach puberty, friendships tend to be reshuffled, based on which kids are leaping ahead into teenaged behaviour and which need to stay kids a little longer. If there's a grade seven move to junior high, that adds another "social shake-up" that is both exciting and scary. It can be painful when children are left behind by their faster-maturing friends, and they may need both tactful understanding and encouragement to find new friends who share their interests.

It's difficult to directly help kids with friendships at this age, but parents can still provide important support. Welcoming your child's friends into your home and helping her get to her friends' homes shows that you value her social life, and provides her with the opportunity to cement budding friendships. Equally important is offering an understanding ear when things go wrong. Finally, continue to make it clear that *you* like your child for who she is—not for the clothes she wears, her athletic prowess, or the group she hangs with.

BEST FRIENDS: KIDS TALK ABOUT FRIENDSHIP

t's easy to feel insulted. Your daughter arrives home from school and brushes past you (without saying hello!) to call her friend. "Well, you wouldn't understand," she tells you when she hangs up the phone. When you announce your plans for an exciting family vacation, your son insists that he won't go without his best friend. "It just won't be any fun without him," he says.

Despite appearances, you are still important to your preteen. But as your child moves toward adolescence, her best friend becomes more than just someone to play with. She is someone to stay up late with at a sleepover or to take off with on a bike to search for new secret hideouts. Perhaps most important, a good friend is someone who can accompany your child through the emotional minefields of puberty while we parents, in spite of all of our good intentions, can really only watch from the sidelines.

Eleven-year-old Ryan Ninabar says, "Friends are people you can trust, people you can rely on, someone you care about and like to spend time with."

Ten-year-old Laura Boulding adds, "If I didn't have my best friend, I'd be really lonely. I wouldn't have anyone to talk to and share things with. If you have a true friend, it means you fight sometimes, but then we figure out why we fought and go on being friends."

"If you went through life without good friends, what would be the point?" says Colin Mulheron. "I don't have any brothers and sisters, so without friends I think I'd be pretty lonely."

Talking about the more private side of growing up is only one aspect of friendship at this age. Colin finds his friendships add a lot to his experience of school: "I like people who are funny. And it's best if you are in the same class, so you can pass notes and talk when the teacher's not looking." He adds, more seriously, that a good friend in your class can help with homework, too.

Friends also provide some protection from the harsh realities of schoolyard life. Laura says, "We look out for each other. There's a guy at my school who bothers everyone—he's so mean—and he jump-kicked me in the stomach. I was really hurt. And my best friend went and got help. I do the same for her, to try to help her."

Some relationships that begin at this age are wonderfully rich and long-lasting. Tara Perkins, 17, first met her friend Lisa when they were both 10. "We just liked each other right away—not that we had the same hobbies or anything, but we're the same kind of people. We even made up our own secret language." Tara and Lisa are now in grade 12, and are still very close. "It's nice to have a friend you've known for so long that you're completely comfortable together and don't have to worry about what you're going to say or do. I think we'll be friends for a long time."

Although most friendships at this age are same-sex, treasured friend-ships can cross gender lines too. Anne Smith says, "My son Adam, who is now 12, has had a girl for his best friend since he was quite young. They are both creative, imaginative kids who have always played really well together."

And other children have told me firmly that gender makes no differ-ence in friendships. "I have a boy who has been one of my best friends since we were both little," says Laura. "We always invite each other when we have parties. I find that the boys who are my friends treat me like a boy—they'll play rough and tackle me. But that's OK."

Colin says, "I have a best friend who is a girl—no, she's not my girl-friend. She really is a friend, just like Jeremy and Matt are my friends."

And what are these kids' tips for children who want to make new friends? Laura's advice is to "just go up and talk to someone. Be their friend, tell them things, ask them to do things with you."

Ryan thinks parents can help, too. "Family friends can be best

BOYS AND GIRLS COME OUT TO PLAY

It's true that cross-gender friendships can thrive in this age group—especially among "old friends" who know each other through long-standing family or neighbourhood friendships rather than the schoolyard. Preteen romance is not unheard of, either. But most close preteen friendships are same-age and same-sex, sometimes quite rigidly so. And while individual exceptions abound, there are nevertheless commonly observed differences in boys' and girls' social styles:

- Boys tend to do things in groups—the more guys, the more fun. Informal sports and active games are still popular in the schoolyard. After school, most boys like to have a concrete activity to share— whether computer games or rollerblading. Preteen boys often have a fairly fluid group of friends, with no strongly preferred friend. If Josh can't come to a movie or sleepover, Ryan will do just as well. Better yet, get both to come!

- Girls are more likely to have a "best" friend, with whom they prefer to spend most of their time. (Although the preferred friend may change fairly frequently.) They are often seen on the school playground in pairs and trios. They spend more of their free time "talking," and less in active play. Parents often note more bickering and hurt feelings among girls, which is perhaps reflective of their more intimate and demanding friendships.

- Late in this age group—often around grade seven or eight—the dynamic changes and kids start to develop a mixed-gender group of friends. At recess, touch football is abandoned in favour of standing around in a clump, talking and teasing each other. Mixed group activities like dances, parties, or excursions to the movies become part of kids' social life, and some experiment with dating. But comfortable same-sex and "best" friends continue to be very important.

friends. If your parents like the other kid's parents, you might like the kid. So that's a good way to make new friends, by going with your parents to visit people."

While they do appreciate a certain amount of input from parents

DEVELOPING FRIENDSHIP SKILLS

Like many experts, Mary Manz Simon, author of *How to Parent Your Tweenager*, advises that it's best not to get too involved in the everyday ups and downs of our children's friendships. But she does suggest that if parents help their kids develop good social skills, they will have a better chance of forming satisfying friendships.

How can we teach good social skills? Manz Simon suggests a large part of it is providing the opportunity to practise—with people of all ages. Babysitting younger cousins, talking with a neighbour, visiting grandparents, or meeting your co-workers, says Manz Simon, all increase a child's social experience and "can boost her confidence as she develops relationships with those people who are so important to her, her peers." Shy children may need more direct adult help, perhaps with role-playing what to say on the phone or in finding an activity that eases the pressure of a first get-together with a friend.

about choosing friends (Ryan says, "Kids should remember that your parents are looking out for you, they want you to be happy"), they don't want their parents to become too involved. Colin says: "I choose good friends. But sometimes you make mistakes while you're getting to know people. That's how you learn."

THE TROUBLE WITH FRIENDS: PEER PRESSURE AND OTHER PROBLEMS

en-year-old Jenna was planning her birthday party—and she was in tears. The problem? She had a good friend in the neighbourhood who would be expecting an invitation, but that friend didn't really "fit in" with Jenna's group of friends from school. "She had never worried about that before, just invited whoever she wanted," observes Jenna's mother, Hailey Cross. "But this year she agonized. The party wouldn't go well, her friend would be uncomfortable. She didn't come right out and admit it, but I think her real fear was that her school friends would think less of her because of her friendship with this other girl."

Jenna's party dilemma is not so unusual, says Sue Benjafield, a parent worker with the Toronto Board of Education and instructor of their classes for parents of preteens and teens. "It's common for kids this age to have different groups of friends that, by and large, don't mix. Friends from gymnastics, friends from school, friends in the neighbourhood..." And, she adds, while friendship groups are still less defined and more flexible than they will be in the teen years, "they do sometimes get cliquey. Girls, especially, can be quite possessive with their friends."

In the preteen years, the social stakes definitely go up. "Friendship takes on greater significance as children start leaving the safety of their homes and trying to increase their autonomy," explains Benjafield. "Their friends provide a support group, a sense of belonging."

The importance of being part of a group (even if it's a group of two) leads to new pressures to *look* and *act* like your friends. The ten-year-old who rarely combed his hair and threw on whatever clothes were at the top of his drawer becomes the eleven-year-old whose undercut hair has to hang just right, who rejects one T-shirt after another at the store for reasons too obscure for an adult to understand. "My ten-year-old son, Matthew, is starting to get the social pressures," observes his father, Jim Levine. "I took him to get new running shoes, and out of the blue it was Nikes or nothing. He mousses his hair every morning. He mainly hangs out with a group of male friends now, but a few of his friends are going out with girls, and I think he's starting to wonder if he 'should' have a girlfriend, too."

As parents, we want to support our children's friendships. We make their friends welcome in our home, we do chauffeur duty, we back up their participation in sports, choir practice, or Scouts. But when problems arise, we wonder how much we should—or can—influence their social life. "Most of the time, kids need to sort things out for themselves," suggests Benjafield. "But parents need to recognize the importance of children's friendships and how difficult the process can be. Without being too controlling or interfering, we can support our kids with lots of active listening, and by helping them develop their own strategies for dealing with tough situations."

Declining an unwanted friendship is a social skill that even adults find difficult, so it's small wonder that kids are sometimes less than gracious about it. "Groups of friends may use teasing and insults to solidify their boundaries and exclude other kids," acknowledges Benjafield. We can take a stand on this kind of cruelty, she says, by reiterating the basic family values we've been teaching all along, saying something like: "You don't have to be friends with Sam, if you don't want to. But it's not okay to be mean to him. *All* people deserve respect."

When your child is on the receiving end of this type of rejection, it's painful for the parent, too. Anne Smith, a mother of three children, recalls, "My daughter Rachel had a best friend in grade six, seven, and eight—they spent almost all their time together. Then another girl came along, told Rachel's friend a lot of lies about her, and the friendship ended. I'd really thought Rachel and the other girl would be friends for life. I just wasn't prepared for that kind of nastiness and malevolence."

Important though it is to a child's development, there's no denying

DEALING WITH BULLIES

It's hard to say which is more painful—having a child who is the victim of bullying, or discovering that your own child is bullying other children. Either way, more and more experts are advising that the worst thing adults can do is to turn a blind eye and expect kids to handle the situation on their own. Bullying can go on for years without adult intervention, and the retaliation kids fear from "tattling" on a bully rarely occurs if the adults involved take the problem seriously.

What should you do if your child reports being bullied? If the situation is not extreme, you might be able to coach your child on assertive behaviours that can defuse the tension (hitting back is rarely a successful strategy, and may lead to heightened aggression). But if your child is unable to deal with the problem herself, or is in actual danger, enlist the school's help. Most schools are taking playground violence very seriously these days, and many have programs or protocols in place to deal with such incidents. Your child may be more open to such intervention if you can secure a promise to keep her identity secret (e.g., the bully can be told "several children have reported to us that you have been...")

For valuable advice on helping both bullies and victims, check out *Battling the School-Yard Bully*, by Kim Zarzour, Today's Parent/HarperCollins, 1994.

that peer influence is not always positive. One of the toughest dilemmas for parents is what to do (if anything) when we are uncomfortable with our child's choice of friend.

Karen Berger's nine-year-old, Emma, prefers spending time with one close friend. But this year, a series of "best friends" in her grade three class have moved to a different school, leaving Emma at loose ends. "It's been quite difficult for her," observes Karen. "But now she's made friends with a girl in grade four, and this friendship is difficult for *me*. This girl is ten going on sixteen, while Emma is still very much a kid. I see some of their discussions going right over Emma's head, and her being introduced to things that are way too old for her."

Of course, you won't necessarily *like* all your child's friends. But it's a different matter if a friend's activities or home situation really worry you. Mary Manz Simon, author of *How to Parent Your Tweenager*, suggests that parents sometimes do need to step in, in order to protect a child's safety or well-being. Start with a realistic assessment of the risks and of your child's maturity and judgement, and then look for a solution that still respects your child's friendship.

"Emma recently invited her new friend for a sleepover," recalls Berger. "We had arranged to drive her back at a certain time the next day, but when we got to her apartment, there was nobody home, and no note to say where her mother was. I didn't get the impression that was unusual. So later I said to Emma, 'I think that Zoey is allowed to be home by herself—but you're not. So if you want to get together on the weekend, I'd like you to invite her to our house.'"

For Jenna's mother, Hailey, the discomfort lay with her own daughter's behaviour, but the question—whether and how to get involved—was the same. "I understood Jenna's concern about the party, but I couldn't condone hurting a good friend's feelings. We talked for a long time, over a few days, wrestling with this thing. I pushed her a little, talking about how it's nice to be part of a group, but it's still important to stand up for what's right. Finally, Jenna said she'd like to have a different birthday celebration with her friend, outside of the party. So they went to McDonald's and a movie together, just the two of them. It cost us a little bit extra, but I thought it was a reasonable solution."

As the teens approach, there's a kind of shuffling of the social cards that starts to occur. Kids are maturing at different rates. Their interests change. They may move to a junior high school. Inevitably, there will be some hurts and losses, as well as new pleasures and excitement, as their friendships evolve. You can't kiss them better, any more than you can make friends for your child. But your support is still important. And so are your car keys.

IF YOU CAN'T TAKE THE HEAT...:
INSULTS AND TEASING

h ey, butthead, get your ugly face out of that bathroom. What are you doing in there anyway, counting all your zits? That could take all morning." "Well, I have to get my stuff finished before you come in and stink the place up."

It's just another loving interchange between my sons, Dan, 15, and Jeremy, 12, during the early-morning rush to get ready for school. While this kind of talk can be hard for parents to listen to, I can tell from the tone of this conversation that my boys are clearly enjoying trading insults.

Debbie Prentice, whose sons Kevin and Sean are now 14 and 13, says, "Smart-aleck insults and banter can be a way of communicating for preteens and teens. I think it's harmless, a way of laughing at yourself."

Both her sons are pretty immersed in hockey, and Debbie notes that "a lot of teasing and insulting seems to go on in hockey. If somebody makes a mistake, the others will really razz him—but they insult the kid who scored the winning goal, too."

In fact, Debbie feels, teasing in the preteen years is often a sign of affection. "Not only with their close friends—the boys tease the girls they like, too."

Natalie MacNaughton's husband, Sandy, likes to "wind the kids up" as Natalie describes it. "He teases them by saying the opposite of what he means, and I've noticed that my nine-year-old son, Willy, is already teasing back the same way." But while Sandy's teasing is all in fun, Natalie has darker memories of being teased as a child.

"I was the middle of three children," she says, "and my siblings joined forces to torture me throughout my childhood. My mother would just tell me not to cry or I'd get teased more." As a result, she

TEASING AND SIBLINGS

Teasing among friends on an equal footing tends to stay pretty good-natured, and it can certainly be that way among siblings too. But often—especially if there is a large gap in ages—teasing can become an ugly way for an older child to prey on a younger sibling's thinner skin.

"Sarah, at 12, is heading into puberty, and she has become quite caustic and critical of just about everyone," sighs her mother. "And Ellie, my seven-year-old, is so hurt by her put-downs. She doesn't have the perspective to shrug it off and say, 'Oh, she's just like that these days.' She takes it really personally."

Your preteen may not want to listen when you explain that the kind of teasing that's enjoyed—or at least tolerated—among his peers is unfair to a younger child. But it's a message he needs to hear, anyway. Shared banter is one thing; having fun by hurting someone's feelings is quite another. Even if you can't stop it completely (and you probably can't), both children should know that you find "verbal abuse" unacceptable.

Is the younger child always the victim? Uh-uh—look at all the things an adolescent has to be sensitive about: breasts, pimples, body hair, first girl- or boyfriends. A mouthy eight-year-old can wreak a lot of embarrassment on a shaky new-teen ego. Again, a good rule of thumb about teasing is how much it upsets the "victim." If it hurts, it's not OK.

generally tries to intervene whenever she hears her children teasing or insulting each other. "I remind them that their words can hurt."

Jennifer Pearson also has unpleasant memories of being teased as a child. "I never found it funny. Most of the teasing was connected to my appearance because I was overweight as a child, and the comments really hurt. I would respond by calling them names, too, and we'd hurl insults back and forth. Later, when I got home, I'd cry."

How can a parent distinguish between the "all in fun" teasing that Debbie describes and the taunting that causes the kind of pain Jennifer experienced? Marie Haldane, a parent-resource worker with Information Children in Burnaby, BC, says: "Teasing can be difficult to respond to or to challenge because it's often an indirect attack—hiding meanness behind humour." If a parent confronts a child who is teasing in a hurtful way, the response is likely to be "I was just kidding."

Haldane points out that with close friends and siblings, the teasing is a two-way street, an easy give-and-take that is often an expression of confidence in the relationship. Like my sons, the kids rib each other precisely because each knows the other will understand. But for a sensitive child, a child who is already dealing with some emotional problems, or one who is being teased or insulted relentlessly, teasing can easily become hurtful. That's why Haldane suggests that both parents and kids try to avoid it. "It's easy to let this pattern of communication become a habit, and we feel families should look for more respectful ways of communicating."

Jennifer finds that teasing is more often a problem at school than at home. "There was an incident, when Sean was nine, of a whole group of kids picking on an East Indian boy," she says. "I believe it was racially motivated. That kind of thing has to be promptly stopped."

As Sean says, when you're this age, "The important thing is being part of the group." The funny insults and teasing jokes between members of the group bring them closer together, and "the mean stuff happens to outsiders."

Natalie MacNaughton is also concerned about teasing at school and how it is handled. "When I've helped out at school, I've noticed that the teachers tend to treat teasing and taunting between girls as insignificant, but quickly reprimand or punish the boys when they tease each other. I also worry that when kids are told not to react to teasing that upsets them, they're being taught to hide their feelings and I'm not sure that's a good thing."

Haldane believes it might be more constructive to suggest that our preteens react to mean-spirited teasing with a calm assertion like "I don't really think that's funny." Sometimes that will be enough to take away the teaser's satisfaction.

Teasing and insults continue to be a part of the social life of most preteens; some have, in fact, turned it into an art form. But the line between teasing that's amusing and teasing that hurts is a fine one, and parents may need to step in at times to keep things on the positive side of that line.

TEASING: HELPING KIDS COPE
For some children, teasing is a big problem. These may be sensitive kids who are more easily hurt by the "normal" digs of this age-group, or they may be kids who are subjected to cruel teasing because of their weight, race, or other differences. Some tips on how to help:

- Don't add insult to injury. Don't try to "toughen her up" by teasing her at home, too, or appear to side with her tormentors ("Well, maybe if you practised more at home, they wouldn't call you a klutz!"). She needs her home to be a refuge, and you to be her ally.
- Listen and accept his feelings. Children's feelings can be very intense, and they don't tone them down in the telling as adults often do. But try not to respond with, "It can't be that bad," or "You shouldn't feel that way." He won't be able to move on to problem-solving if he's full of stifled anger.

How should your child respond to teasing? It has to be something that feels doable to her. So brainstorm together. Ask her how she thinks she might want to handle it next time. Some possibilities that have worked well for other kids:
- Ignore it. This really does often work, but she should know that it will take time, and the teasing might even get worse at first while the other kids test her resolve. It's also *hard* to ignore teasing. It might help if she counts silently to herself, walks away from the

teasers, changes the topic, concentrates on breathing slowly and deeply, or uses a physical distraction like flexing and releasing her muscles.

- Tell them to stop. This can work well when it's a thoughtless friend who is teasing: "That makes me feel bad and I don't want you to say it any more, OK?" It's less likely to be effective on a hostile playground, but kids often feel better just for having been able to say it. Coach your child to aim for "quiet and firm," rather than angry and desperate.

- Deflect it with humour. It takes quick thinking and a quick tongue, but humour is often well accepted by other kids. A caution—some kids adopt a self-deprecating humour ("I'll insult myself before anyone else can") as a survival tactic—which erodes their own self-esteem. Humour works best when it doesn't hurt anybody— including the child using it.

"YOU'RE INVITING WHO?" MIXED PARTIES

idway through the school year, sixth-graders Matt and Danny are talking about parties. "We used to rollerblade, or play soccer, or, like, wrestle around. Now at parties we listen to music or watch a video. I guess we're not so rowdy," grins Matt.

There's been another dramatic change, too. The last few parties they've been to have included both girls and boys. That change has raised a few parental eyebrows, especially considering that only a few short months ago, the girls in Matt and Danny's class wouldn't even *sit* beside the boys.

"At the beginning of this year, the girls all totally hated us," says Danny. "It was so bad our teacher didn't want to take us on an overnight camping trip she'd planned—'cause we'd just fight. Now they're all inviting boys to their birthday parties. Everyone is."

"It's happening at around 12 these days," confirms Mary Gordon, administrator of parenting programs with the Toronto Board of Education, "depending on the dynamics in their class."

Admittedly, there's something disconcerting about these suddenly more "mature" parties. "It does make parents nervous," says Gordon. "For many, it means suddenly seeing your child as a sexual being for the first time. You wonder, what does it mean? How closely do we have to chaperone?"

But while we're looking ahead to the days when our kids might be necking in the corner (and let's face it, those days are not so far away), Gordon reassures parents that at these preteen parties, "the kids have nothing serious on their minds at all. It's still pretty innocent."

So when our kids reach the stage of wanting a mixed party, Gordon encourages us to go ahead and host it. In fact, if you have room, she thinks having the whole class is a great idea. "It's a little easier on the child," she says. "If you're inviting everyone, you don't have to come out and actually say which boys you like! And it's a great chance for parents to meet both your child's classmates and their parents. You know, you lose that once kids start high school."

Shelly Hunt's daughter Michelle, aged 12, recently invited her class of 15 to a birthday party. "She wanted it to be an 'adult' party," says Hunt. "She asked me, 'What do adults do?'"

Gordon points out that party etiquette is changing at this age, and has some tips to help things run smoothly:

Avoid anything babyish. "They want an evening party now, and nothing like theme cakes or loot bags. A gag gift for each guest or something like that would be better."

Supervise—discreetly. "You want to establish some ground rules from the start," says Gordon. "Kids generally don't want parental participation any more. Make it clear that you *will* be there, keeping an eye on things...but try not to be too obvious." At Michelle's party, the kids played truth or dare at one point, with the emphasis on the *dare*. Hunt says, "I kept popping in, saying, 'Nobody has to do anything they don't want!' And a couple of kids did speak up and refuse the dare, saying 'I don't want to do that.'"

Have an activity or two available, just in case. "These first mixed parties can be a little awkward, and sometimes the option of an outdoor scavenger hunt or a game of Pictionary helps get things going," says Gordon. "Once we got permission to have a campfire at a local park, and that was a big hit." Even a video of animated shorts might save an awkward moment. Danny remembers that at his first mixed party, hosted by a boy, "One girl arrived before any of her friends and she just sat in the corner looking embarrassed until they arrived." Hunt

THE SLEEPOVER PARTY

Sleepover parties (same sex, of course) are extremely popular with the pre-teen set. Not that there's likely to be much sleep involved. Even kids at the younger end of this age group, given the right dynamics, can stay awake far later than any parent wants to! Yet experienced party hosts say that it is possible to give your child a wing-ding of a sleepover and still get a little sleep yourself. Here are some tips from the trenches:

- Have plenty to do. "You need lots of things to entertain them," says Cindy Foulon, whose three kids range in age from nine to fifteen. "One activity won't appeal to them all, and it's the kids who aren't interested in what's going on that get wild." Nicki Clark, mother of three girls and organizer of three ninth-birthday sleepover bashes, has it down to a semi-science: "A friend of mine makes craft kits, so I get one for each girl. We have a variety of games and lots of dress-up clothes. I get one really good, 'hot' video, and one boring one for bedtime. Last time, instead of a bunch of candy in the goody bags we got a magazine for each guest—and that kept them going for the night."
- Be clear about your bedtime limits. They aren't going to be asleep by nine, or ten, or even eleven. But they needn't be up all night, either.

stresses the value of having alternatives in mind: "They're not all going to agree on what to do. At Michelle's party, most of them watched a movie but three kids thought it would be too scary for them and so they played cards."

Once mixed parties become the norm among a group of kids, those parents who have qualms about them (and some do) have a difficult call to make. "Everybody else gets to!" is the battle-cry of youth, and as parents we need to have the confidence to stick to our own best judgement. But preventing kids from sharing in the social development of their peers is not a step to take lightly. It's reasonable—and wise—to insist on basic safety precautions, like parental supervision, but

Kids will usually respect reasonable limits, firmly stated. "We have lights-out at midnight," says Nicki, "and they're usually all asleep by one or one-thirty. At least, anyone who's still awake is quiet enough not to disturb us!" If you want the kids to settle down at night, it pays to set the stage a little. Ten-year-old boys are not going to admit they're scared by a horror movie—in fact, they'll clamour to watch it—but they may well need to break the spell with loud, rowdy play before they can face going to sleep afterwards. A quiet, non-scary pre-bed activity is a better bet.

- Expect a mess, but don't get stuck with it. "Basically, it's got to be in a room that can be totally destroyed," says Nicki. She's only half joking. That many kids, that excited, staying for that long, can't help but leave an impressive trail behind them. At the Foulons' house, one of the conditions of having a sleepover is that the party boy or girl helps clean up the next day.
- Plan for a day of rest. You're all going to be tired. Try not to be heading into a busy day of hockey practices, piano recitals, or demanding dinner parties!

before forbidding your child to attend or host a mixed party, you might want to consider this reminiscence from Helen Finlayson, mother of 12-year-old Andrew:

"I remember I was in grade seven when I got my first invitation to a mixed party . . . and I was the only one not allowed to go. So I stuffed my skirt into my baseball mitt, and told my parents I was going to the park to play ball with friends, and went to the party. Only the next day some friends of mine guilted me out about it so much that I went to my parents and confessed. I guess I thought that they'd say, 'Thanks for being honest with us,' and negotiate something. Instead they hit the roof and I got into deep, deep trouble. And you know, I clearly remember thinking, 'That's the last time I tell you anything.' And it was!

"I think about this experience now that Andrew is heading into his teens," adds Finlayson. "I want him to feel he can talk to me—and I think these first tentative steps toward new social relationships are so important."

There's nothing wrong with socializing between the sexes, and mixed activities in a group is a far cry from dating. Parents of boys, especially, may even appreciate the somewhat civilizing effect girls may bring to a gathering. "Friendship is one of life's greatest pleasures," says Gordon. "This is a wonderful opportunity to foster that." Danny puts it rather more pithily: "It's no big deal. And it's better than hating each other, isn't it?"

A DIFFERENT DRUMMER: THE NERDY KID

omputers, comics, eating, and sleeping. That's my life." This from 12-year-old Colin, a self-described nerd. Does it sound like a lazy, unstimulating life? Not if you understand the uncompromising intensity and scope of Colin's two current passions.

"Colin approaches comics like adult collectors or art critics do, not like a kid," says his mother, Charlotte Everett. "His comics are not light entertainment for him. They are serious study. He's followed the evolution of certain old superheroes. He's into particular artists and writers. His room is total chaos, his schoolwork is messy—but his comic collection is immaculate."

Lots of kids like computers and comics, but Colin takes these interests well beyond most of his peers. "He has no interest in the mainstream stuff," says Everett. "So it's rare that he really connects with another kid around this."

What is a nerd, anyway? Like all social labels, the word is subject to various interpretations. But ask around, and common themes do emerge: strong, even obsessive interests of an intellectual or technological bent; and a disregard (either conscious or oblivious) for the social conventions and pressures that drive most preteens.

"They're in another world," explains my own 12-year-old son.

"Do you dislike them?" I ask, remembering guiltily a girl from my own grade-five class who was smart as a whip, into geology and studiously avoided by us all.

"No, not necessarily," he replies. There's his friend Jeremy, for instance, who goes to school every day with his vest pocket crammed full of pencils, knows passages from *Lord of the Rings* by heart, and once faxed me two pages of instructions for correcting problems I

MAKING CONNECTIONS: FRIENDSHIP THROUGH LIKE-MINDEDNESS
These kids need to have their interests supported, but their best bet for good friendships also lies in connecting with kids who share their passions. That may be as simple as signing him up for a computer programming course. But "nerdy" kids aren't always keen to join group activities, and in smaller towns the range of available programs may be narrow, so it can take a lot of searching and experimentation to find the right fit. Some ideas:

- Add a group component to individual lessons: If she's a keen pianist, perhaps her teacher could arrange for some ensemble or duet practice.
- Look for informal channels. What if your child is into something like Magic Cards? You're not going to find a course through your local board of education! But ask around. You might find that there are Saturday afternoon tournaments at the local card and comic shop, for example. (And yes, you may have to attend yourself the first few times and lurk in the background, just to make sure it's safe and appropriate.)
- Go farther afield. You may not find a local program that appeals. How about a specialized summer camp (there are camps emphasizing everything from science to visual arts) or a father-son trip to a Star Trek convention? A one-week friendship with a kid you really "clicked" with (especially if you can exchange e-mail or letters through the winter) can make a big difference to a lonely kid.
- Use the Internet. Yes, you have to set up some safety rules (see "Welcome to Cyberspace," page 109). But this is an excellent tool for kids with specialized interests that gives them access to information, resources, events, and people from around the world. It's not a great route for finding a personal friend (although enduring pen pals are not unheard of), but it does bring a sense of community: There are all these people who like birdwatching as much as me!

was having with my computer. "He's a nerd, and I like him a lot."

"I'm offended by the label," says Wayne Campbell, a former science teacher and co-founder, with his wife Carol, of Hila Science Camp near Pembroke, Ontario. Still, he acknowledges that Hila, with its hands-on, in-depth approach to science, attracts a lot of kids "who seem to stand apart for some reason. They are driven by their interests, no matter what."

Campbell thinks it is "tragic" that these kids get so little encouragement to pursue their talents. Preteen culture, with its rigid ideas of what's "cool" and what isn't, pushes kids to fit in or face rejection. The nerdy kid is more likely to be joked about than admired by her peers. "It takes a great deal of courage to reject these pressures," Campbell reflects.

Campbell doesn't think the community at large does much to support these kids either. He cites a case where a child he knew came second in a Canada-wide science fair. "That's a pretty impressive achievement—but it was nearly impossible to get any media coverage for this kid in the local papers. Yet at around the same time, I saw this big spread on a boy who came third in a regional shotput competition. So what does that say about what we really value?"

"I think adult role models are really important for these kids," says Charlotte. "Colin went to a computer camp where they met a guy who's been involved in developing innovative new software. That guy was a nerd, too—but he was a cool, fun, successful nerd. He didn't fit in by pretending he wasn't smart; he found a place where his smarts were valued. An adult who can be a bit of a mentor gives a kid a glimpse of what his future might be."

"Parents can help by finding resources, programs, and people who share, value, and validate the child's interests," confirms Campbell. "An adult in the field, or a program that can show her the link between whatever she's working on and its eventual applications—whether that's playing in an orchestra or designing robotics—can be a key experience. These kids want to do something real."

While special programs can also help young people find like-minded friends, their social life at school may be more of a challenge.

"What makes the difference between an unusual kid who is fairly

"FEMININE" BOYS, "MASCULINE" GIRLS: BENDING GENDER LINES

Victoria was an athletic, active girl who spent most of her elementary school recesses playing soccer or touch football with the boys. The boys accepted her in their games, and she was well-liked by the other girls. By grade six, though, things were becoming awkward. The boys didn't seem to take her participation seriously, and teased and joked around when she tried to join in. Her girlfriends told her she should "grow up," which seemed to mean spending recess standing around in a huddle, talking and giggling. Victoria didn't feel like she quite belonged in either group.

Nobody worries about "tomboys" any more—at least not until near puberty. But there is still pressure on girls to act more "feminine" as they grow older, and friendships can be strained when girls resist that pressure. Happily, the emphasis in recent decades on opening up options for girls and women has paid off. Active, exuberant girls can usually find both friends and physical challenge in a range of sports programs—Victoria, now 12, plays on two hockey teams and has met lots of other girls like herself.

Life can be a lot tougher for the boy who is drawn to more traditionally "feminine" activities. Adults tend to be much more uncomfortable with this trait (and quicker to associate it with homosexuality), and other children soon pick this up. "The social stigma is much bigger," confirms Alice Charach, a psychiatrist with the Hincks Centre for Children's Mental Health in Toronto. "These boys are at risk of being bullied at school, unless the school has a culture that accepts and makes allowances for differences."

Again depending on the school culture and their specific interests, boys who play more easily with girls may come into their own in their mid-teens. In high school, they may be involved in a band, acting in musicals, or editing the school newspaper—all great activities that comfortably mix the sexes, arguably in a more "normal" social environment than that of the locker room.

Our children are who they are, and like what they like. Our job is not to change that (as if we could!), but to help our kids discover their own talents and joys, to support them on their path even if it's at times a difficult one. Our gender biases haven't disappeared yet—but we owe it to our kids to keep working on it.

well accepted at school, and one who is rejected or persecuted?" muses Charlotte. "Good social skills are part of it, but maybe another part is just luck—how much tolerance of diversity there is in that environment, whether you happen to rub a popular kid the wrong way."

Even if they are welcomed into the fold, "nerdy" kids may be too individualistic to fit into a group. "Colin is a sociable kid," says Charlotte, "and he does have good friends. But they are all *individual* friends. They don't hang around together as a group. And, you know, I worry about that. They'll be heading into high school soon, and there is a kind of protection you get from being part of a circle of friends."

It's true that, as parents, we can't help but feel protective of our children's vulnerabilities. But Campbell reminds us that by recognizing and nurturing their strengths—in this case, a passionate mind and enormous self-direction—we can help our kids shine. "We had a boy in our camp who was totally into space travel. He's a graduate student now, working on fusion propulsion. These kids are the ground-breakers of the future. We should be applauding their efforts like crazy."

ADOLESCENCE APPROACHETH

Getting Ready for Puberty

YOUR NINE-YEAR-OLD COULD BE YEARS away from puberty...
or it could be just around the corner. Experts and parents alike
observe that early puberty does seem to be more common than in pre-
vious generations, so it's important for both you and your child to be
prepared. In fact, even kids who are "late bloomers" need to under-

stand the changes their friends are going through and that it's OK for them to be a bit behind.

Adolescence, of course, is about more than physical changes. As the teenage years beckon, most kids develop an emotional "edginess" that can sometimes strain family relations. Picture a toddler with an attitude, and you've got one side of adolescence. Add in the risky temptations these kids are beginning to face—from smoking to sex—and it's easy to see why some parents view their children's transition to adulthood with a certain amount of dread.

Try not to fall into that trap. There is plenty to enjoy about teenagers! These kids are bright, passionate, interesting people who still love you (though they may not always act like it) and still need you (though they may not always admit it). Let your preteen know you are proud of the way he's growing up—whether he's taking it fast or slow—and are confident you can both handle the changes to come. But no one will blame you if you secretly cherish these last few years of childhood, either!

PUBERTY 101: WHAT TO EXPECT

ne moment Amy is this sweet little kid who wants to crawl into my lap for a cuddle and a hug," says Rowena Kirby about her 12-year-old daughter, "and the next minute she's yelling at me because I went into her room and moved a piece of paper and invaded her privacy."

Amy's rapidly changing moods can be hard to deal with, Rowena confesses, but they're all part of the normal changes that go with puberty. "She's wearing a bra now, but she's very self-conscious about it," says Rowena. "She doesn't want people to know that she's wearing one. She'll stand in front of the mirror pulling her T-shirt tight and checking from all angles to make sure nothing shows. And she's always asking me about the changes she sees in her body—wanting to know if she's normal."

Amy, who has just turned 12, is in the middle of puberty. Her breasts have begun to develop and she has grown pubic and underarm hair, but hasn't yet begun menstrual periods. "We've talked about menstruation," says Rowena, "and she still thinks it sounds pretty disgusting, but she's getting used to the idea. And of course some of her friends are already having periods so that's helped to prepare her."

Puberty is the process of change and physical maturation that takes boys and girls from childhood to adolescence. It can begin as early as age nine for some girls; boys are usually two or three years later. The average age of the first menstrual period for girls in North America is 12.4 years, according to the University of Toronto publication *Health News*, but some girls will begin as early as 9, while others will not menstruate until they are 16. Boys develop body hair, a deeper voice, and other changes between 10 and 18 years of age.

Most children learn the physical facts of puberty during health classes in school. But they may not be prepared for the sometimes overwhelming emotional changes—and parents can have a tough time dealing with them as well.

Nick Graham, a single father whose five children live with him, says that his daughter Emma seemed to change more as puberty arrived than his sons have. "I think that's because girls mature physically at a younger age; they are almost forced to be more adult because of the way other people respond to them," Nick says. "She became more interested in her appearance, in clothes, things like that."

His sons, on the other hand, have treated the arrival of puberty as more of a joke. Nick remembers that Emma was pretty distressed when she developed acne and that contributed to her moodiness. Similarly, his oldest son Aidan "went through a stage at about age 12 when his hands and feet grew enormously" before the rest of his body caught up, but Nick found that Aidan wasn't especially worried about it.

As for his younger sons: "They think pubic hair and stuff are kind of funny. Sean, who is ten, told me the other day that his 'pits smelled now' so he's started using deodorant. They joke about shaving, and I remember finding the whole thing terribly embarrassing, so I'm glad they're able to take it less seriously."

One area Nick is serious about, though, is sexuality: "I really try to downplay the joking around sexuality. The boys laugh about masturbation, for example—saying their friends do it, though of course they insist that *they* don't. But I think it's important not to trivialize sex."

As a single father, Nick has found it easier to talk to his sons than to Emma. "I think it's more appropriate for her to talk to her mother about sexual aspects and about concerns like menstruation. She sees her mother frequently and I think they communicate well about these topics. But she doesn't come to me with her questions the way the boys do."

Nick feels that preparation is essential to helping kids—and parents—get through the challenges of puberty. "Let them know about the changes and what to expect before they get there. When puberty

PUBERTY RESOURCES FOR KIDS

Changes in You & Me: A Book about Puberty, by Paulette Bourgeois and Martin Wolfish, MD, Somerville House Publishing, 1994. Two editions: *Mostly for Boys* and *Mostly for Girls*. These matter-of-fact, reassuring "his-and-hers" Canadian books cover body changes, questions about sex, and puberty in the opposite sex—and each also includes a welcome chapter on handling the tough decisions that all teens face.

It's Perfectly Normal: Changing Bodies, Growing Up, Sex and Sexual Health, by Robie H. Harris, Candlewick Press, 1994. The text of *It's Perfectly Normal* is quite similar to other contemporary puberty books, but the illustrations give it a lighter tone that kids will appreciate. Many are humorous and/or quite explicit, and there is a definite emphasis on showing all sizes and shapes of bodies.

The "What's Happening to My Body?" Book and *My Body, My Self: The "What's Happening to My Body?" Workbook*, by Lynda Madaras (et al.), Newmarket Press (Canadian distributor General Publishing), 1994–95. Two editions of each: *For Girls* and *For Boys*. The *What's Happening* series is well written and thorough, but it's the workbooks that really stand out as a different, more "interactive" approach to puberty education. The combination of information, true/false quizzes, tips, fantasy conversations, and personal input is sure to engage most kids.

What's Happening to Me? A Guide to Puberty. This 30-minute animated video is tastefully produced, using a combination of facts and humour. A good resource to watch together.

actually arrives, it may be too embarrassing for them to talk about."

Parents should remember, too, that each child is an individual and may reach puberty at a different age, or progress through the stages at different rates. It's important to reassure the little girl who develops breasts at age ten that she's normal, and to let the boy who shows no signs of maturing at 14, that his turn will arrive.

What's more, kids can't escape the development of sexual feelings and interest that arrives with the hormonal and physical changes. This is another area that is important to talk about, preferably before it happens. Nick says: "The children began learning as preschoolers how babies are made and the significance of sex, and over the years we've also talked to them about moral responsibility. At puberty, all that suddenly takes on a new importance—it's like reality hits." Rowena remembers Amy telling her about a dream she'd had and didn't fully understand. "As she described it to me, I suddenly realized that it was really an erotic dream. In some ways, she's just a little kid, but those feelings are already starting."

Puberty is a time of sorting out new relationships between parent and child as the family copes with both physical and emotional changes. It's exciting and sometimes stressful, but it's important for both of you to remember that, despite the ups and downs, this is a positive development in your child's life.

FIRST MENSTRUATION: GIRLS' RITE OF PASSAGE

emember the myths from a generation or two ago? You couldn't get your hair permed when you had your period because it wouldn't curl properly. You shouldn't take a bath or go swimming during your period—showers only. You were putting yourself in danger if you went near a dog—it would know you were having your period and attack you. And all those euphemisms: "a visit from Mrs. McGillicuddy," "my monthly," or simply "that time."

Diane Putnam, mother of three children (two girls, now 15 and 13, and a 10-year-old boy) remembers, too, how many girls had no preparation from their parents before the onset of menstruation. "There was one girl in my class at school who I found in the washroom crying because she was bleeding and didn't know why. She thought there was something terribly wrong with her, that she was going to die."

With those memories in mind, Diane has made a point of telling her own three children about menstruation from early childhood. "I want them to feel that it's normal and natural, so I never tried to hide it from them."

Diane didn't sit down with her children to deliberately discuss menstruation; she simply took advantage of the opportunities that came up. When she bought sanitary pads in the grocery store, her children asked what they were and she explained: "You remember I told you about how each month the blood comes out from my uterus. These pads catch the blood and keep it from getting on my clothes or underwear."

If they saw blood on her underwear or bedsheets, she explained that she was "having her period" and emphasized that it was normal and healthy. "Sometimes they'd be scared if they saw blood—because they associate it with being cut or hurt—and so I really tried to stress that there was nothing wrong."

For Colin Burke, a single father raising his 12-year-old daughter Melissa, discussing an issue like menstruation is more challenging. He can't share his personal experiences or take advantage of the kind of natural opportunities that Diane can. "Sometimes it's hard because I'm not a woman. I don't really know what it's like or what she's going through."

Nevertheless, he feels the close relationship he has with Melissa makes it easier for them to talk about sensitive subjects. His daughter has found her own way of initiating discussions of these topics, Colin says: "I noticed that when she has something on her mind she'll suggest we go for a drive together and that's when she'll ask me questions about things like menstruation or sexuality."

Both Colin and Diane feel that preparation is important, and that it's wise to discuss the changes puberty brings long before they've begun. Remember, too, that girls may begin to menstruate as young as nine years old, and that if your daughter has begun to develop breasts or pubic hair, it is possible that her periods will not be far behind (although there is considerable variation). "And there is more to talk about when it comes to menstruation than just the facts of the monthly cycle," says Diane. "When I was a teenager, we were told that PMS was all in our heads, we were just imagining those symptoms. I wanted to let my girls know that the things they felt—the bloating, the feelings of stress, the cramps—were all real."

While Colin feels that Melissa's health classes at school have given her most of the information she needs, Diane cautions that they can't always be relied on.

"When Amanda had health class, her teacher was so clearly embarrassed by the part on menstruation that he just read it really fast out of the textbook. Later when Amanda's period started one day at school, she went up to this teacher and said, 'I'm having a little problem.' His reaction was: 'Don't talk to me about it, go talk to one of the female teachers.' He made her uncomfortable at the time, but we laughed about it later."

CHANGING OUR ATTITUDES ABOUT MENSTRUATION
What if some boy sees the tampons in my backpack?
What if Sherry tells someone?
What if I don't get to the bathroom on time and there are bloodstains on my pants and *everyone knows?!*
    There is certainly less taboo these days about *advertising* "sanitary protection" products. But when it comes down to individual women, there is still an aura of secrecy surrounding menstruation. Ironically, this can cause a lot of anxiety and embarrassment to girls who not only have to cope with the mechanics of managing their period at school, but also have to pretend they're not! Yes, it's private—but if it were no more private than, say, urinating, it would save a lot of stress. (Imagine feeling free to simply say to some boy, "No, don't throw me in the pool! I have my period and don't want to get the pad all wet!")
    That day may be some time off, but the more matter-of-fact and open we can be in our families about menstruation, with our boys as well as our girls, the less it will be a mutual source of embarrassment in the teen years.

Diane is confident that her son, Ryan, won't have the same attitude. "He knows about it, he hears his sisters discussing it, and I think it will just be a normal part of life for him." Boys need to know about menstruation in a factual, positive way. "My husband, Pete, has been a big help with this, too," Diane says. "He didn't know anything about menstruation as a boy, and he found the whole idea pretty frightening at first. He's determined that Ryan will understand that it's just natural and no big deal."

Colin has also tried to emphasize the normality of menstruation by not making a big fuss about it. He says his challenge is remembering to bring the right supplies when he and Melissa go on holiday together: "It's just something I wouldn't normally think of!"

Even with the best preparation, beginning menstruation can be an emotional time for many girls. Diane remembers, "Even though she knew all about it, and she'd seen her older sister go through the experience, Amanda cried when she had her first period." Why? "Something to do with being grown up now and not feeling ready. It is a significant occasion, and it's not surprising that she felt emotional."

Menstruation is definitely a rite of passage—a major event in a young girl's life—and some families have begun recognizing its onset with a celebration of some sort. A "puberty party" or ceremony is probably too flamboyant and public for most girls' taste, but your daughter may really appreciate a quieter gesture: going out together to a nice (grown-up) restaurant, the passing down of a keepsake from your own mother.

It's important to realize, too, that some girls will respond to this big change in a very private way. So if your daughter seems reluctant to discuss her "news" with you or with other members of the family, respect her wishes. After all, it's not every day that your body changes so suddenly and dramatically.

TALKING ABOUT SEX: NOW OR NEVER!

ids today seem so savvy. With all they're exposed to—from frank educational books to "sex scenes" in movies, they know more than enough about sex by their teen years. Or do they?

Meg Hickling doesn't think so. The Vancouver nurse, sex-education specialist, and author of *Speaking of Sex*, still hears almost unbelievably naive questions and comments from the preteens she teaches. "Many kids will still say, 'Well, you get pregnant when you eat something.' They're stuck at the idea that you have to swallow something to get pregnant, because parents have said that the baby grows in the mother's stomach or tummy. I've had many, many children tell me—especially grades five to seven—'Well, you have sex when you're in love, but you won't get pregnant until you get married.'"

It sounds cute and funny, but at this age such misinformation is just plain dangerous. "I met a 13-year-old girl who got pregnant in grade seven, because her mother had told her 'you get the babies when you get married' and so she thought she could have sex without the risk of pregnancy," says Hickling.

The reality is, children are exposed to a great deal more sexual innuendo, sexual glorification, and graphic sexual images than we were. What they don't always get is the complete, careful information that would allow them to understand their own puberty, have a realistic idea of what sex is about, and make responsible sexual choices in high school. And at least some of that information, argues Hickling, needs to come from you—the parent. "School programs can be good, but they aren't always very good. Some classroom teachers don't feel very comfortable with the subject, and will have restrictions about which questions they will answer. Of course teachers are also constrained by the curriculum and its guidelines about what they can and can't talk about. So children are sometimes left with less than adequate responses to their questions." It's up to parents to fill in the gaps.

"This is a tremendously needy group," adds Hickling. It makes sense. These kids are going through puberty, and have had far more exposure to talk shows, schoolyard gossip, and even pornography (at the very least, the covers at the video store!) than younger children have. They must be full of questions!

But just try to get them to ask. Many children this age have become embarrassed and reluctant to talk about sex, even if they questioned you openly (and relentlessly) as preschoolers. "You have to demonstrate to your children that it is okay to talk about this, and that you are willing to talk," suggests Hickling. "If you wait until they're teenagers they'll just walk away from you."

How to get started, then? "Grab every single teachable moment," suggests Hickling. "You can do it in tiny bits and pieces. When you're driving her to piano lessons, you can pick up on a piece of news that's on the radio and say, 'Do you know exactly what that means?' And you never take the child's answer, 'Yes, I know, let's talk about something else.' You ask the child to tell you what she knows about it. And if she doesn't want to, then you say, 'Well, okay, then, this is what I want you to know about this particular subject.'" When this kind of casual talk is difficult to manage, Hickling offers a last-ditch plan: "Put them in the car, and drive to Buffalo, so that they're captive, and you can talk to them. And even though they groan and moan and say, 'Ahh, Dad, this is so disgusting, and you're a pervert, and I know all this stuff,' you just continue to talk through their (and maybe your) embarrassment."

What do we need to talk about? Hickling outlines a number of key areas:

Their bodies and puberty. Surprisingly, quite a few children still have many questions and worries about puberty changes, in part because it

THE PRIVATE CHILD

It's an age of increasing need for privacy: The child you raised with such casual comfort with the human body suddenly wants you to stay out of the bathroom when he's in the tub and won't come in your room in the morning until you're completely dressed. It's all normal, and sex educator Meg Hickling says that all we need do is respect our child's heightened sense of privacy and embarrassment.

And keep talking—embarrassment or not. But, she says, "Some children have a very, very private nature. It's part of their genetic makeup." These kids, she explains, may literally not hear information presented at school, "because it's just too difficult for them to cope with this in a big group, and so they actually will tell me that they closed their ears. They didn't hear."

Of course, it's a challenge for parents of these kids to help them learn what they need to know, too. What can you do?

- Keep it short and sweet. Try frequent little private discussions, maybe at bedtime when the lights are out, not overwhelming the child with too much at once.
- Read aloud. Get a couple of really good sex-education books, suggests Hickling, and if the child will allow you to read with him, or aloud, that would be great. It's a little less personal that just talking, so maybe easier to handle.
- If even that's not tolerable, give the child the books. Tell her she can write any questions on a piece of paper if she can't ask you directly. A video—and a private place to watch it—can be another good alternative.

does seem to be happening earlier and parents are waiting too long to initiate the conversation. "One girl told me that she got her period in grade three, and her mom had not prepared her so she had no idea what was happening," recalls Hickling. "So we want them to know totally about their bodies—how they work, how to take good care of them, how they are going to change—and to be so self-confident that they won't hesitate to tell their parents and see a doctor if they have a problem."

The mechanics of reproduction. "They need to know exactly what sexual intercourse is all about, and how pregnancy occurs. They need to understand that you can get pregnant the first time you have sex, and that you don't necessarily have to have penetration to get pregnant, that if there is any ejaculation near the vagina, the sperm can find their way in," advises Hickling.

The facts about STDs. Preteens need to know that there are very serious sexually transmitted diseases that can affect anybody. Hickling observes, "There's an element of classism and naiveté to the way children approach this. They may say, 'My friend couldn't possibly have a disease—her father is a doctor, or he's a champion skier.' And they often don't realize that partners might lie about not having an infection, or simply not know."

Your thoughts on teenage sex. "We want them to think hard about whether sexual relations are going to be a good idea for them when they go to high school," says Hickling. TV shows and movies, she points out, suggest that sex is a "normal part of dating." If you feel that sexual activity should be part of a long-term, committed relationship, say so. Kids need to understand that few high-school romances last into adulthood. They need to think about the reality of teen pregnancy and STDs. They need to think about their own maturity: Would they be comfortable going to a doctor and talking to their partner about contraception, for example?

A realistic perspective on pornography. Finally, says Hickling, kids have a lot of questions about what they see (or get told about) in pornographic material. "Children really need to know that real people don't behave, or look, like people do in pornography. They need to know that the pictures are enhanced: Nobody has a body that good! And they need to know that having a sexual relationship doesn't mean you have to do all that stuff in the movies: that in a sexual relationship you have a choice, and you never have to do anything that you don't want to." And don't be afraid to reinforce a little the natural revulsion most pre-teens feel towards sexual activity: "When they say, 'OOOOh, gross!' I say, 'Good, I'm glad you think it's gross. Sex is for adults, not children.'"

Hickling acknowledges that some parents are so uncomfortable they are simply unable to talk with their children about sex. "They may have sex abuse in their own background, or have grown up in homes that were so repressed that it still feels really sinful and dirty to talk about it. So my suggestion for these parents is to find out how good the school program is, and, especially if it is not adequate, provide their children with some really good books and resources."

But one way or another, our kids do need us to help them figure out the increasingly compli-cated subject of sex. Here's another funny/sad story to illustrate the point: Hickling tells of one grade four boy who came home from school and told his mom he was dying of AIDS. "And the mom just burst out laughing. But the boy became hysterical and upset, and insisted it was true. Finally the mom asked, 'Brian, do you know how you get AIDS?' 'Yes,' he answered. 'All the kids at school were talking about it, and I heard the commercials on TV. They said if you don't wear a condom you'll get AIDS. And, mom, I haven't been wearing a condom.'"

It's not fair to make kids needlessly afraid they are dying of cancer or AIDS—or to allow them to blithely take risks unaware of their danger—just for a lack of knowledge. It's time to talk.

RECOMMENDED READING

Speaking of Sex: Are You Ready to Answer the Questions Your Kids Will Ask? by Meg Hickling, RN, Northstone Publishing, 1996.

HOMOSEXUALITY: HELPING KIDS
UNDERSTAND SEXUAL ORIENTATION

 fter we'd watched a made-for-TV movie about AIDS, my 11-year-old son turned to me and asked, "Mom, I know what men and women do when they have sex, but how do two men have sex?"

I gulped and did what I always do in these moments—try hard to remember how my parents dealt with the same situation. It only took me a second to realize that my parents didn't have to deal with this particular situation. When I was young, homosexuality was never discussed. At age 11, I had no idea it existed.

As the gay-rights movement and the dramatic impact of AIDS have increased the public's awareness of homosexuality, it has become a topic parents can no longer avoid. But that doesn't mean discussing it with our children is always easy.

Alex McKay, research co-ordinator of SIECCAN (Sex Information and Education Council of Canada), says, "Homosexuality is part of the broader topic of sexuality, and it's something many parents are uncomfortable talking about. Parents may be able to give children the basic facts about how babies are conceived without too much discomfort, but they find it hard to talk about desire, attraction, and the feelings of sexuality."

He adds that parents are sometimes concerned that discussing homosexuality with children will influence the child's sexual orientation. "We know from decades of research that a child's sexual development has nothing to do with being educated about the diversity of sexual feelings that people have."

Parents who are very uncomfortable with the topic should spend some time educating themselves, he suggests. The library or your public health department should have materials on sexuality that will give you the information you need to talk to your children.

Miriam Kaufman is a Toronto paediatrician and the mother of two children she is raising with her partner, Roberta. Kaufman frequently speaks to groups of children about sexuality and is often asked to help educate other physicians as well.

"I think when your child asks you about homosexuality, you need to stop for a minute and think about why the child is asking you these questions. Usually it's for one of three reasons: She's heard or seen something and is basically looking for information; she is feeling 'different' and wants to know if it's OK; or she's been exposed to some homophobic comments and wants your reaction." A casual question—"Oh, was someone talking about that at school today?"—can help you clarify your child's concern.

When children are looking for basic information, she suggests simply giving them the facts without much commentary. But if you're not comfortable getting into the mechanics, Ruth Miller, sexual health educator with the Metro Toronto Public Health Department, says a parent could answer a question like my son's, about how two men have sex, this way: "People can be sexual with each other in many different ways. Just as men and women who are attracted to each other like to hug and kiss and touch each other's bodies, so two men or two women might do the same things." She also suggests that parents might answer a question like this by asking the child, "What do you think?" He may already have some ideas and could just need you to confirm or correct them.

Kaufman points out that even at this preteen age, many kids are wondering about their own developing sexuality. "Many gay adults remember feeling 'different' at this age. I don't think they recognize at nine or ten that they are gay; it's more in retrospect that they realize what their feelings meant." She also reminds parents that it's quite common for children in this age group to have strong attachments to members of the same sex without becoming homosexual.

McKay feels parents can help their children by letting them know that sexual orientation is not an either/or proposition, but that there are a variety of ways that people feel. He says you might explain that most people are attracted to and fall in love with people of the opposite sex, but some have these feelings about people of the same sex, and some for both sexes. Kaufman adds, "I would stress that the gender of the person someone loves is not as important as the fact that they have love in their lives."

Helping children avoid homophobia is an important issue for many parents. "I think we need to be much more aware of this kind of discrimination," says Kaufman. "There has been a backlash recently around politically correct language, but language can be very powerful, and there are a lot of derogatory terms for gays in many children's vocabulary."

She points out that if a child told a classmate to "f— off" he would probably be sent to the office, but that if the same child called another a "fag," the name-calling would likely be ignored. Children often don't know what it means to yell "queer" at another child—they only know it's seen as an insult. McKay agrees: "I would make it very clear that just as we don't stigmatize people because of their race or religion, we don't call people names because of their sexual orientation. When you call someone a fag or other name, it's the same as a racial slur. Children need to know that these words hurt people."

Kaufman finds that homosexuality is sometimes best understood by children when it can be related to someone the child knows—a friend, relative, teacher, or celebrity who is gay. This gives the parent the opportunity to point out the ways in which the person is "just like us" as well as being different in this one aspect of her life. "All of us have similarities and differences, and we need to build on our connections and accept our differences. That's the message I'd like to give all kids."

My son absorbed the frank information I gave him about how gay men have sexual relationships, and then asked, "And what do two women do?"

I suspect I'll be answering questions about sex for several years yet. But I'm learning not to avoid these tough topics, to talk openly about our friends and acquaintances who are gay, and to be able to say to my kids, quite honestly, "If you grow up to be heterosexual or gay or bisexual, I will love you exactly the same."

"MIRROR, MIRROR ON THE WALL, AM I BIG OR AM I SMALL?" PRETEEN BODY IMAGE

t just four feet tall, nine-year-old Ty is dramatically shorter than most of his classmates. He doesn't seem to care about it much, though—except when people mistake his best friend for his big brother.

Serena, at 11, is very tall and already well into puberty. She's quite self-conscious about her new figure, and usually wears bulky sweatshirts to school, because she feels like "everyone stares at me."

At ten, Martin thought he was "fat" and needed to go on a diet. But now, at 12, he has grown dramatically, and is the first of his friends to sport broad shoulders, a deep voice, and the beginning of a moustache. He's pretty happy with the way he looks, although he often has trouble getting kids' rates at the movies.

"Body image is a really big issue for kids in this age group," confirms Miriam Kaufman, a paediatrician at Toronto's Hospital for Sick Children and co-author (with Teresa Pitman) of *All Shapes and Sizes: Promoting Fitness and Self-Esteem in Your Overweight Child*. No wonder. At an age when they're quite concerned with fitting in and "looking right," the unpredictable pacing of puberty means their growth rates and body shapes are all over the map.

In particular, says Kaufman, "Many children are afraid of becoming fat. They've learned that it's 'bad' to gain weight. Yet it is normal to put on weight in preparation for the growth spurt in puberty, and for many kids that's frightening. It doesn't feel normal, it feels like their bodies are out of control."

Allie Hearn's daughter, Chloe, is ten years old and showing a new awareness of how she—and other people—look. "She's more concerned

EATING DISORDERS: WARNING SIGNS
Although we tend to think of them as adolescent girls' diseases, eating disorders like anorexia and bulimia can affect preteen children, and can affect boys as well as girls. These are serious, sometimes life-threatening illnesses that require professional support. Dr. Miriam Kaufman suggests there may be cause for concern if your child:

- is throwing away her school lunch, hiding food, or showing other signs of secret dieting
- is getting obsessed about what he eats
- is actually losing weight
- exercises compulsively, especially after eating
- talks a lot about hating how her body looks

In most cases the first step would be a visit to your family doctor or paediatrician, who might refer you on to a program or counsellor.

about styles and fashion and make-up, and she spends a lot of time looking at herself in the mirror," observes Allie. "She comments about people who are skinny, her friends being skinny. A few times she's said something like, 'I'm fat.' But it doesn't get past me. I don't berate her for saying it, but I tell her, 'That isn't anything you need to worry about. You're beautiful no matter what.'"

While "average" is an elusive concept at this age, Kaufman points out that children who are at either end of the "growth and development scale" may be especially prone to a poor or anxious body image.

Early or late puberty. Kids are really self-conscious about puberty anyway, but when they are among the first or last, it's all heightened. "I feel like a freak" is the complaint (voiced or secret) of the early or late bloomer.

"Chloe's going through puberty now, and several of the girls she knows are ahead of her. They're just ten, which doesn't seem very old, does it?" notes Allie. It's understandable, then, that kids sometimes have a little trouble keeping up with their own development: "Chloe's body is changing, and this is a point of tension," says Hearn. "Her hair gets dirtier faster, and she has body odour on occasion. She needs to shower more often. But I have to really force her into the shower. These body changes are happening, but she doesn't want to change her behaviour yet."

Taller or shorter than average. "There is a bit of a gender split here," observes Kaufman. "More often boys worry about being too skinny or too short. Girls can feel more self-conscious about being really tall. Some kids agonize about this, while others seem oblivious."

One problem for these kids is that other people may actually treat them as though they are younger or older than their real age. "There's a tendency to expect, even pressure, the tall child to be more mature, and to treat the small child as a little kid when he needs to grow up like everyone else," cautions Kaufman.

Overweight kids. Overweight children may have their own concerns about how they look, but often they must also contend with painful teasing from their peers: "Kids are still really being taunted about being overweight," says Kaufman. She regrets that "adults tend not to intervene with this type of teasing as quickly or firmly as they would stop racial slurs or physical aggression."

What can parents do to help our preteens feel more comfortable in their own skins?

"I think we have to start by really watching how we talk about ourselves and other people. We have to stop criticizing our own bodies all the time, or judging other people by their body size and appearance," suggests Kaufman.

"Chloe rarely sees me fretting about my appearance, or putting a lot of time or energy into it," says Allie. "But those messages are every-

THE OVERWEIGHT CHILD

Children, like all human beings, have a range of body types, and some have a definite tendency to store more body fat. But in our society, being thin is valued and being overweight can have painful emotional "side effects," from social rejection to low self-esteem. How can parents help an overweight child?

Authors Teresa Pitman and Miriam Kaufman, MD, address just this question in the book *All Shapes and Sizes: Promoting Fitness and Self-Esteem in Your Overweight Child* (Today's Parent/HarperCollins, 1994). Among their suggestions:

- Make sure your child knows you love and accept him the way he is. Overweight children need just as much physical affection, admiration, and companionship from their parents as other kids—more, if they're not getting much from their peers. Don't let his weight become the focus of your relationship.

- Don't encourage dramatic dieting. Children should not be losing weight at this age—a better goal would be to stabilize and grow into the present weight—and in any case dieting doesn't work in the long term, even for adults.

- Do encourage healthy family eating. While kids should not be going hungry, there are "non-punitive" changes you can make to lower your overall fat intake and boost nutrition.

- Find enjoyable ways to boost activity levels. Overweight children may not feel comfortable (or get much playing time) in organized sports, but there are many other options. Go skating, swimming, biking together, have dog-walking be one of her chores, let her try out a more individual sport like karate.

- Help him find strategies for dealing with teasing, if that's a problem (see "Teasing: Helping Kids Cope," page 50). If he gets teased a lot, and it really upsets him, you might try enlisting the school's help in reducing the teasing and/or a counsellor to help him cope.

where—and I think this is the time when girls start realizing that they're going to be appraised on their looks. We were watching a TV show the other day—I don't remember what it was—but there was something really overt and I turned to Chloe and her friend and I said, 'Wait a minute. That's not all there is. Being a girl is not just about having boys look at you.' I said, 'You should choose to look good for yourself and no one else. You role is not just to please the eye of a boy.'"

Kaufman also urges that we avoid passing on messages to our preteens that dieting is good, or that calories are bad. "On the whole, it's not safe or healthy for kids to lose weight before their growth spurt. If a child says she's going on a diet, parents should say no. This is one place where a firm directive is appropriate. Dieting is almost never a good thing for a kid to do, and if it is indicated, it should be medically supervised."

Children need to understand, instead, that it's important to feed themselves well so that they can stay healthy and strong through puberty, and that a calorie is just a measure of energy in food—energy that they need to grow. "We want to encourage healthy eating," suggests Kaufman, "but in terms of *including* the things we need more of, like fruits and veggies, not by forbidding foods or counting calories."

In early puberty, children are heading into major body changes. They are growing, literally, in all directions—and their proportions can, in fact, look a little peculiar for a while if some body parts grow out of synch with the others. It's normal, under the circumstances, for kids to feel uncertain about their appearance or a bit anxious about what the end result of this work-in-progress will be. But most preteens take it all in stride, and parents can help by encouraging them to focus on being healthy and active, rather than a certain size or shape.

"BUT I HAD A SHOWER LAST WEEK!" WHAT'S WRONG WITH WASHING?

h e used to love having baths when he was little," says Helen Parry about her nine-year-old son, Scott. "Sometimes he'd spend ages in the tub, either playing with his toys or just relaxing in the water. But those days are long gone." How does Helen account for the 180-degree change in Scott's attitude toward personal hygiene? "I'm starting to think he has some kind of soap phobia!"

Here's her description of her struggles to get Scott to keep clean: First, she reminds him several times that he needs a shower. He mumbles, "In a minute," and continues what he's doing. Finally she gives an ultimatum: Either he has a shower or he can't come shopping with the rest of the family. He heads for the bathroom but, Helen says, "He's in and out so fast that I can't believe he can be any cleaner than before he went in." She hears the water turn off and arrives upstairs just in time to stop him from putting on the (very dirty) jeans he's been wearing all day.

As they go downstairs, Helen notices that while Scott's hair is definitely wet, it shows no signs of having been shampooed. When questioned, Scott looks surprised. "You didn't tell me I had to wash my hair, too," he says.

Silvia Wynter's two sons, Austin (nine) and Chad (eleven), are equally unenthusiastic about keeping clean. "Just recently," Silvia says, "I sent Chad up for a shower and he actually cried, he was so upset. Even when the shower was running I could hear him grumbling and cussing at me under his breath. He acts like I'm sending him to be tortured." And when Chad and Austin emerge from the dreaded shower, they leave the bathroom in total disarray, with wet towels, discarded clothes, and water everywhere. "I think this is my punishment for forcing them into the shower."

ONE EXTREME TO THE OTHER
"I used to drag him out of bed at the last minute, and he'd eat breakfast and stumble onto the bus without even brushing his hair," says a bemused mother. "This year, he suddenly has to shower every morning. And he actually gets up 15 minutes before everyone else so he can do it before we all have to use the bathroom!"

Some kids go on being grubby right through the teen years. But plenty suddenly transform into the best-groomed people on earth. Many teens of both sexes have a horror of being seen with oily hair, the slightest body odour, or any article of clothing that isn't straight out of the wash. That means the years to come are likely to bring some heated negotiations to book shower times and laundry schedules, and to establish ownership rights over blow-dryers and other personal grooming equipment.

"You can't have too many bathrooms," one father of three girls once said to me. That said, many of us can and do struggle on with just one. But you might want to use this "low-maintenance" stage to save up for a high-capacity water heater...

Silvia says that she and her husband are very conscious of cleanliness and can't understand how they ended up with two grubby boys who have to be strong-armed into the bath. "Sometimes I'm afraid I'm going to give Chad a complex. I always seem to be asking him if he's had a shower, if he washed his face, if he washed his hands."

Why are many kids this age so devoted to being dirty?

Toronto teacher Roseann Boulding says that every year she and her colleagues have to speak to a couple of boys about their need to wash more often. The problem, she says, seems to be less prevalent with girls. "I think some of it is that we raise boys differently than girls, as a society. A boy who is a bit grubby is acceptable and his friends probably won't even notice. A girl who hasn't washed is much more likely to hear about it from her friends, and to feel like she should do something about it." Either way, your child's attitude is bound to have a lot to do with what his friends think. After all, at this age, fitting in with peers is more important than ever before.

Helen Parry feels that for her son, "it just takes too much time to be clean, and it's not high on his priority list." She's noticed that, often, Scott can barely pull his pyjamas on because he hasn't dried himself properly and he'll arrive downstairs with dripping wet hair that hasn't even been towel-dried. "I think he's afraid that if he takes ten minutes out to shower he might miss something really exciting."

Joanne Tee, a social worker in private practice in Hamilton, Ontario, says that this disdain for cleanliness can be a child's way of exercising his growing independence. Parents are often there to ensure that their young children stay clean, but as kids mature, personal hygiene becomes an area where they—quite rightly—want to make some of their own decisions. She advises parents, "Remind yourself that this will pass, and then relax your standards a bit. Insist only on what is essential for good health. You need to be letting go a little each year as your children grow up, and this stage can be good practice in backing off."

This lack of interest in being clean generally ends when kids discover the opposite sex. Silvia can already see the beginnings with Chad. "He's starting to be concerned about his image now, and wants to wear after-shave or cologne." This hasn't yet induced him to embrace the joys of a good shower, but, says his mom, she thinks she can see the light at the end of the tunnel.

DRINKING, SMOKING, AND DRUGS: GETTING THROUGH TO OUR KIDS

ou can't help but notice them as you drive past the local junior high: little clumps of kids huddled together on the sidewalk, puffing away. You glance back at your ten-year-old reading a comic book in the back seat, and wonder if she'll be part of this crowd of smokers in a few years.

Smoking, drinking, drugs. As Katie Kidd, program co-ordinator at the Halton (Ontario) Alcohol and Drug Assessment, Prevention, and Treatment Program (ADAPT) points out, "It isn't a question of *if* your child will be exposed to or offered these things. It's inevitable. You can't avoid it or protect them. What you can do is prepare them."

For some kids, these forbidden substances are seen as a shortcut to maturity. "It's a very vulnerable time," says Cheryl Moyer of the Canadian Cancer Society. "We know that one major danger period is when children make the transition to junior high or high school. They want to seem grown-up, and smoking seems like a way to do it."

Besides wanting to look cool, many girls start smoking in order to lose weight. Allison, now 17, took up smoking five years ago. "I was getting fat and some of my friends told me that smoking would help keep the weight down. It's true, too. If I'm hungry, I'll have a smoke instead."

Few parents are comfortable with the idea of their preteen or young teenager experimenting with recreational drugs of any kind. But how to dissuade them? Lectures on the hazards of tobacco, alcohol, and drugs are rarely effective, and can even backfire, according to Peter Cowden, an adjunct professor of educational psychology at Niagara University in New York. "For some kids, the dangers of drugs are part of the attraction. They want to do dangerous things. They want the thrill, the risk." And as Moyer points out, "Preteens and teenagers are not very inter-

A BROADER APPROACH TO PREVENTION
Recognizing the broader problems that underlie serious drug use is the basis for the Lions–Quest Canada program, which is offered in many schools across Canada. The program's focus is "Life Skills Education" and children in grades six to eight use the "Skills for Adolescence" curriculum.

The obligatory sections on the risks of drugs and alcohol and how to say no to peer pressure are included. But these are embedded in an 18-week program that focuses on broader life skills: building self-confidence, communicating effectively with others, managing emotions, strengthening relationships, solving problems, etc.

The benefits, according to program secretary Fay Anonthysene, go beyond the prevention of drug use. A survey of 500 schools across Canada using the program found that 95 percent saw improved problem-solving by students and 77 percent reported reduced discipline problems.

Will the program reduce the rates of early drug use? We can't know for sure. It certainly seems likely, though, that kids who can make good decisions, solve problems creatively, and exercise self-discipline will be less vulnerable to negative pressures of all kinds.

ested in long-term hazards. Lung cancer and heart disease are too far in the future for a healthy young person to imagine."

Other kids are not attracted to the dangers, but are trying to ease some emotional pain in the only way that seems to work. Cowden explains, "They usually know the risks, but they don't care. They just want to get through today."

Cowden advises, "Simply educating kids about the dangers of drugs won't prevent or end drug use. It just isn't enough." He points out that eight studies have found the Drug Abuse Resistance Education (DARE) program, offered in many schools across the US and Canada, to be simply ineffective. While the students who had been through the program knew more about drugs, they used drugs at the same rate as those who had not participated in DARE.

The best protection from all kinds of drug abuse—whether that drug is marijuana, alcohol, or tobacco—lies in "good, solid parenting," according to Kidd. "Parents often believe that they have no influence on kids, but that just isn't true. Parents should maintain their faith about how important they are to their children, even as their children move into adolescence."

Cowden encourages parents who are worried about their preteens to focus on these important parenting areas:

Consider the kind of example you are setting. Tobacco and alcohol are the drugs most commonly used by teenagers—and most commonly used by their parents. If you drink, do you use alcohol responsibly? Moyer points out that statistically, children of smokers are much more likely to smoke themselves. She suggests keeping your home smoke-free even if you do smoke—when you inconvenience yourself to protect him from second-hand smoke, it reinforces to your child that you believe cigarettes are hazardous. Kidd adds that it's important to demonstrate problem-solving that doesn't involve resorting to the quick fix of a drink or medication.

Emphasize helping your child to feel loved and respected. Your child may be under a lot of stress, especially as puberty arrives. His growing independence doesn't take away the need for support from parents. "Children learn to treat themselves and their bodies with respect when their parents treat them with respect. It sound so simple, but for many people it's hard to do," explains Cowden. Moyer adds that in her focus groups, she was surprised to find how important parents' opinions actually were to teens and preteens.

Help your child develop social skills and competence. Children who are involved in a number of activities have the opportunity to get to know more people and to become more self-confident. They have less

A LOOK IN THE MIRROR

Get ready, 'cause it's coming:

"So, Mom, did *you* ever smoke a joint?"

"Did kids drink at parties when you were in high school?"

Honesty or evasion? When Charlene Giannetti and Margaret Sagarese polled a group of parents for their book, *The Roller-Coaster Years*, 98 percent said they would give their children honest answers to questions about their own past. Yet the authors question whether honesty is always the best policy. They summarize some of the issues:

- Will lying cause me to lose credibility and trust with my child?
- Will he dismiss as hypocritical my attempt to dissuade him from doing what I did?
- Does admitting past indiscretions give tacit approval for repeating the behaviour?
- Do kids really learn from their parents' mistakes?

No one can tell you what to do with a judgement call like this, but the authors do make the excellent point that you can be honest without going to the other extreme and "telling all." It's okay to keep some parts of your past private (or private until she's older), just as you keep some other aspects of your personal life private.

need to rely on drugs to have fun. Kidd says, "The kids with passive lifestyles, who overdose on the entertainment of movies, TV, and video games, are at greater risk of abusing drugs or alcohol. Kids need involvement—activities like sports, music, and dance. Help them find something they can be passionate about."

Encourage your child to "give service to others." Cowden cites this as an important way to boost self-esteem. "When kids do things for others, they feel more valuable."

Cowden does believe that it is valuable to share realistic information about the hazards of all drugs—from caffeine and nicotine to alcohol, steroids, and PCP. But he stresses that it isn't knowing about drug risks that protects children from becoming drug abusers: "The everyday things you do as a parent to help your child feel valued and cared for are much more important than any lecture on the evils of drugs."

PARENTS ARE SO EMBARRASS-ING! WELCOME TO THE PEANUT GALLERY

 want to go see that new movie with my friends," 12-year-old Whitney announces. "Could you drive us?" "Actually, I've been wanting to see that movie, too," says her father. "Maybe I'll come with you."

Whitney is horrified. "You can't come with us! You can't. Just drop us off and we'll call you when it's over."

As she stomps out of the room, her father, confused, turns to his wife. "When did we stop being cool and turn into geeks?"

It can happen to any parent. One moment your little one is permanently attached to your leg, unwilling to even let you go to the bathroom alone. The next moment she doesn't want to be seen with you.

Parent educator Dianne Banks, of Oakville, Ontario, says, "The first thing parents should know is not to take it personally. It's not so much about you as it is about the stage of development of the child."

Children moving into adolescence (and this stage can begin as young as 11 or 12) often begin taking steps to establish their own independence. The parent who was once seen as all-knowing and wonderful is now subject to closer scrutiny, and even minor faults suddenly become glaring problems that cause the kids acute embarrassment. As the opinions of their friends and peers become more important to them, they worry about the impression their parents are creating.

Banks remembers children who were very upset by their father going to the store in his work clothes (mechanic's overalls). "They weren't even going with him, but they were afraid some of their friends would see him dressed like that and know he was their father." Many mothers have been quite offended when their entire wardrobe is suddenly dismissed as "disgusting" by a preteen who has recently discovered fashion (the same daughter who spent her

WHO'S EMBARRASSED NOW?

If kids are easily embarrassed by their parents, the feeling is certainly mutual at least some of the time.

- "I let him buy a T-shirt with his favourite band lettered on the front. It wasn't until I got a call from the school that I learned it had a swear word on the back—he'd gone out the door with a sweatshirt on so I wouldn't see it."
- "Amy and her girlfriend started laughing in the restaurant I took them to, and they couldn't—or wouldn't—stop. They went on so long, and were so loud, I finally took my food to another table."
- "I asked Jacob to clear the table when we were visiting my mom, and he just looked at me indignantly and said, 'Why should I?' My mother was shocked (visiting manners were ingrained in us at an early age) and I was totally mortified—even though at home it wouldn't be a big deal."

No words of wisdom here—kids are not always going to act or look the way we'd like, and sometimes that will be embarrassing, end of story. This is a good time to repeat to yourself, "My child is a separate person, not an extension of myself."

Of course, if something is really bothering you, you might look for an opportunity to bargain: "No, Marian, I guess I don't *have* to roll my cuffs up like that. I tell you what. I'll unroll my cuffs when I'm out with you, if you get rid of that big wad of gum. Deal?"

first ten years wearing grubby, mismatched sweatshirts and pants).

"Think back to when you were that age," Banks says, "and you'll probably remember feeling some of the same things. Didn't you think your parents dressed weird and drove 'uncool' cars and treated you like a child in front of your friends?"

Other factors may make this stage more complicated. When Alyce married Michel Fregault, her daughter Erin was 11. Michel was anxious to establish a good relationship with Erin, but she often complained that he was embarrassing her.

"She said that she hated it when I dropped her off at school and gave her a hug in front of the other kids. She said they laughed at her. Well, I never had a child before, I didn't know that was embarrassing for 11-year-olds. So I stopped hugging her in public," Michel says.

As Michel found, this is a tricky age for establishing new relationships. His step-daughter's reaction may have had as much to do with adjusting to the new family as with her stage of development. But even parents who have been with their children since birth find that they go through many changes as their offspring move through puberty and beyond. "Parents say 'my child's body has been taken over by aliens,'" according to Banks. While they once felt capable of predicting the child's behaviour, now they're often caught by surprise. Again, Banks reminds parents that these changes are a normal part of growing up.

So how can you deal with a child who doesn't want to be seen with you?

"You need to be respectful of their feelings," says Banks. "Don't hug and kiss them in front of their friends if they ask you not to, and don't reprimand them in front of other children." Dropping the child off a block away from school (instead of at the front door) is another request that's easy to satisfy.

But other complaints shouldn't be taken too personally. Your preteen doesn't have to like your new haircut or approve of the music your choir sings. "Continue being yourself and having your own values," says Banks. "Don't let these comments hurt you, because they're not really about you—just stand back and don't get emotionally involved."

She reminds parents that trying to dress and act like a teenager is a mistake and not likely to win their child's approval anyway. "Your child doesn't need a 40-year-old friend who is trying to pretend to be 15. He needs a friendly parent who is comfortable with himself."

If you have had a good, strong relationship with your child, this stage is likely to be intermittent and temporary. While your son may be humiliated because you car-pooled his friends "with country music playing on the radio—how could you?" a week later he may be proudly bringing those same friends home to sample the brownies you made.

As Banks advises, "Keep telling yourself—this too shall pass." It really will—it just might take a few more years.

PRETEEN PLEASURES
From Play to Pop

Brenda Cooke

WHEN IT COMES TO PLAY, YOUR PRETEEN has the best of all worlds. His growing co-ordination and cognitive abilities open up all kinds of possibilities: ping-pong or snorkelling, chess or charades. He easily moves from fantasy play to sophisticated computer games, from active play on a climber to detailed work on a craft or model. This age is great for parents, too, since there are now so many activities you can both enjoy. You can go biking or cross-country skiing together, play Pictionary or cribbage on an even footing, find a movie you both like. Don't miss this chance to share your "playtime." It will pay off not only in fun, but in a stronger parent-child relationship.

As kids head into the teen years, their leisure time gradually takes on a new flavour as toys and dramatic play are left behind in favour of new, more sophisticated interests—like pop music, fashion, computer games, or athletic pursuits.

But don't clear out the toy cupboard just yet. The same 12-year-old who is loudly scornful of a younger sibling who "still plays with dolls," may well get out her old Barbies that same night for a private visit in her room. Meanwhile, her twin brother will have a wonderful time playing with his younger cousins' transforming action figures—toys he wouldn't touch within sight of his friends. The chance to revisit and enjoy "younger" toys and games provides, as one ten-year-old explained, "a relief from the pressure of being grown up all the time."

POP CULTURE RULES! CAN WE MAKE PEACE WITH KID KULTURE?

••

ylie eats, lives, and breathes Hanson," says Kathy Cunningham about her 12-year-old daughter. "Every inch of wall in her bedroom is covered with photos and posters of these three guys. She talks about them all the time. She gets on the Internet and checks their Web site and sends e-mail to other people who are also obsessed. I have to admit, I've had it up to here with Hanson."

Chandra Reid's sons, Ben, 11, and Aaron, 9, have a different obsession: the WWF. "They love watching wrestling," Reid says, "and I can't stand it. I just think it's so fake and so violent. I can't believe it's not bad for them. But they love it. When they're not watching, they're acting out the fights with their wrestling figures."

If you have no idea who Hanson is (a rock band), or are not sure what WWF stands for (World Wrestling Federation), don't feel bad. You're just a typical adult. Perhaps your child and her friends have latched on to another part of popular culture that leaves you as bewildered—and vaguely concerned—as Kathy and Chandra. You overhear them on the phone, recounting the latest movie or TV show in exquisitely tedious detail, or see them standing around on the sidewalk intensely trading the vital statistics on the pop band of the moment, and wonder (like parents before you) if your child's brain is turning to mush. Oh, for the days when they were interested in dinosaurs!

"I guess the need for kids to have their own culture, things that they like that their parents don't like, has been around for a long time," Kathy says. "I remember the girls who went to Beatles concerts and screamed and fainted. I wasn't that obsessed, but I did like the Beatles and my parents didn't."

In some ways, it's probably harder for kids to find a way to express

A DELICATE BALANCE: THE PARENTS' RESPONSE

Whether we like 'em or hate 'em, when we respond to our children's pop culture passions we also have to bear in mind a preteen's need for respect, independence, and, yes, parental guidance. It's a tricky balancing act. Let's look at a few examples:

- Twelve-year-old Max is a fan of the grunge band Nirvana. He's learning guitar, and likes playing along to his Nirvana CDs. Max's dad, wanting to support his interests, helps him find chord charts for his favourite songs and brings home a band biography. Well and good, but then he starts learning the songs himself, and soon he knows more about Nirvana than Max does. Max mysteriously loses interest in Nirvana, and before long announces that he has become a "death metal" fan...

- Stephanie (11) begs her parents to let her watch "South Park," a late-night cartoon they really don't approve of. They ban it for a while, but it soon becomes apparent that she's seeing many taped episodes of the show at her friends' houses, anyway. So they decide to watch it with her, and "educate" her on why they find it offensive. After a few weeks of this, Stephanie heads back to her friends, telling her parents, "I don't want to watch it with you. You're just trying to wreck it for me!"

Should we, then, never get involved in our children's interests, or discuss our concerns? Of course we should!

A shared interest can be a point of real connection with our kids: ten-year-old Joseph and his mom are both *Star Wars* fans, for instance, and

their separateness from adults these days. The 12-year-old who announces he loves Our Lady Peace might be dismayed to discover his parents are also fans and are happy to educate him about the songs ("Did you know that the song *Julia* is about John Lennon's mother?"). Pretty deflating to a kid trying to be cool. Or consider the ten-year-old who adores "The Simpsons" because of the show's "authority sucks" attitude—until he finds himself laughing at the same jokes as his parents. As a result, these preteens might end up going a bit farther afield

Joseph really enjoys the time they spend reading the sequel novels together or quizzing each other on car rides from a *Star Wars* trivia book. But we need to be aware that at a certain age, kids need some interests of their own, and to be alert for signals that we're overdoing it.

Similarly, it's important to set reasonable limits and to discuss our concerns with aspects of pop culture that make us uncomfortable. Your kids need to know that you don't condone racist or sexist messages in music videos, or that the glorification of violence in movies disturbs you. But don't, as Kathleen McDonnell writes in *Kid Culture*, let your expressions of concern degenerate into the "Sneer Tactic...a predictable stream of snide comments." Our kids deserve the same respect for their likes and dislikes as we expect for ours, and if we do decide to let them watch a show or participate in an event (even if we have qualms about it), then we should do them the courtesy of allowing them to enjoy it.

to find an aspect of popular culture that they can call their own—enter "Beavis and Butthead"! (For more on this, see the box "A Delicate Balance," p. 102.)

Or they might stay pretty close to home, and just pick out something that drives mom or dad nuts. Chandra Reid's neighbour is a committed feminist who was incredulous when her daughter, at age 11, became fascinated with beauty competitions and started spending hours discussing makeup and fashion with her girlfriends. "It just went so much against her mother's values," says Chandra.

"I think that banning something—whether it's wrestling, Ninja movies, music videos, or beauty contests—just makes it more appealing to kids," says Chandra. "On the other hand, though, you are still the parent. You can put some limits on things."

For example, Chandra allows Ben and Aaron up to two hours of TV each day, and that stops them from "overdosing" on wrestling and music videos (their second-favourite thing to watch). Kathy Cunningham, too, tries to keep some limits on Kylie's Hanson obsession. "She'd spend hours talking with other fans on the Internet or repeatedly checking the Web site, so we have to limit her time."

In her 1994 book *Kid Culture* (Second Story Press), author Kathleen McDonnell says, "Many adults seem locked into a fear-and-loathing response to kid culture. But the main problem I see with this attitude...is that it's a dead end. It takes us nowhere except to become one more in a long line of missed opportunities for dialogue between the generations."

Trying to understand your preteen's fascination with stuff that doesn't appeal to you can help you get a better handle on where he's at. "When I watch the boys play with their wrestling figures, if I can get past the bloodthirsty elements, I can see how they want to root for the 'good guy' and have good triumph over evil," says Reid.

For many kids, pop culture is also a way to fit in and have something to talk about with their peers. Just as adults will make conversation with a comment about last night's hockey game or the latest episode of "ER", so kids make connections with each other through their own culture. At an age when both social circles and social pressures are growing (and when boys and girls are learning to relate to each other in a new way), being able to participate in a conversation about the latest episode of "X-Files" or the hottest CD on the charts offers reassuringly safe ground.

"I think the most important thing is to keep some perspective on all this. I know that one day Hanson won't be so central to Kylie's life—I just wish that day would come quickly!" says Cunningham.

FADS AND FASHIONS: WHAT'S HOT IS COOL

When he was ten, my son, Danny, insisted that most of his clothes have Toronto Blue Jays logos or designs on them. Now he's "too old" for that, and he wants more sophisticated clothing (Nike T-shirts are popular). He's traded in the comfortable sweat pants he once wore on every occasion for loose-fitting blue jeans.

Both of my younger sons are solidly committed to the baseball cap as a fashion statement. Each night when they go to bed, the Cap of the Day is carefully hung over the bedpost, topping a stack of ball caps. In the morning, a new one will be just as carefully selected. They are worn indoors, outdoors, to school—although a few teachers require their removal in the classroom—and, of course, at play.

As children become preteens, following the latest fad and keeping up with the newest fashion suddenly becomes incredibly important. It can be a shock when the child who cheerfully wore hand-me-downs or whatever you picked up at the store abruptly refuses to wear anything that isn't approved by her peers. Parents are often worried about the cost of the current fashions (the most popular item is almost invariably the most expensive) and that their children are too caught up in being "one of the crowd."

Other parents find watching their children begin to make independent choices about what to wear very stressful—they may feel as though they are losing control. "Sylvia's favourite look is like a snapshot of the worst of the early seventies: platform shoes, bell-bottoms, and skintight little T-shirts. I'm sorry, but it does embarrass me when she goes to school looking like this," laments her mom. If this sounds familiar, try not to take your child's choice of clothing or hairstyle as a personal rejection of, or reflection on, your taste. Your preteen needs to feel that she can be her own person, and this is one way to do it.

As Oakville, Ontario, parent educator Dianne Banks says, "Parents should remember that fitting in with their friends is very important to children of this age. Even if you don't find the clothes they want to wear very attractive, if all their friends are wearing similar styles having the right clothes can mean a lot."

Of course, it isn't always possible to buy your child the "in" thing. "If it's something your child really wants, but it's beyond your budget, let him know that you would really like to be able to get it but can't afford to. Perhaps you can work out a way for the child to earn the money, or perhaps it could be a special birthday gift," suggests Banks.

Often, having a few of the "right" clothes will be more important than having many changes of clothing. Dan, for example, has decided he'd rather have a couple of pairs of jeans (which he washes frequently) than the half-dozen pairs of sweatpants that would cost the same amount of money. (See how responsible a preteen can be when he needs to be!) Other kids have been known to limit themselves to their two favourite or newest outfits, even when their closets are full of clothes.

Makeup, jewellery, and hairstyles also become important at this age, particularly (but not exclusively!) with girls. "At a certain point hair dye went through the class," remembers one father ruefully. "The girls seemed to be colouring their hair black, and the boys, including my son, were trying out coloured streaks and stuff. They all looked pretty awful, actually. But I told myself that it was nothing irreversible—in fact Ben's hair washed back to normal pretty quickly, and he didn't bother to recolour it. In the end, it was just something fun to try out."

While a preoccupation with fads, fashions, and fitting in is a normal stage, some parents worry because their children *aren't* interested. Susan Stuart's daughter Mary, age ten, differs from many of her friends in that she seems completely unconcerned with clothes and fashion: "Mary plays hockey and soccer and loves sports. I guess she is more worried about whether her clothes are comfortable than about how they look on

BODY PIERCING & TATTOOS

Baggy pants pulled down to the hips with boxers sticking out of the top? It looks dumb, but you can handle it. Jet-black dyed hair, cut short with a long hank hanging down? You can handle it. Cropped-short lime-green shirt, with a black vinyl mini? You can handle it (just). Pierced navel and a butterfly tattoo? HOLD IT RIGHT THERE.

The coolest parent will have qualms about permanent "body art." And despite your child's hot protests, you do have cause to be concerned.

Here, for example, is what Dr. Laura Walther Nathanson has to say about body piercing, in her book *The Portable Pediatrician's Guide to Kids*:

"Piercing your earlobes is different and safer than piercing other parts of the body. First, your earlobe is just soft skin, and it's out in the open. If you pierce your earlobe and it gets infected, it's easy to see what's going on and easy to treat. But the firm part of your ear, and the nostrils, are made out of cartilage. If you pierce the cartilage and it gets infected, this can be a very serious infection that could even destroy the cartilage and leave a big hole.... That hole is not easy to fix and looks terrible."

Tattoos should be considered permanent, and 12-year-olds are not always capable of anticipating how they'll feel about their decorated skin in a decade. (It is possible to have tattoos removed using either laser technology or skin grafting, but the process is neither simple nor inexpensive.)

When unclean needles are used for either tattoos or skin piercing, there is a risk of hepatitis B or even HIV transmission. Before giving the OK to anything, you should be convinced that needles are either new or (for tattoo equipment) sterilized in an autoclave.

Given the potential long-term consequences, you have good reason to withhold permission from any body-puncturing activity that makes you nervous until your child is old enough to be completely in charge of his or her health. But try to make sure your nervousness is justified, not just a matter of aesthetics. If you're comfortable with one hole per ear, what's so bad about two?

her," says Stuart. "When I threw her old running shoes away, she actually fished them out of the garbage because she said they were more comfortable that the new ones."

Banks assures parents in Susan Stuart's situation that their kids are doing fine. "It's OK to support a child who wants to fit in by wearing the clothes that are in style, but we also need to let our children know that it's OK to be different."

And, of course, Mary's interests may change as she gets older. In a couple of years, she could feel the way 11-year-old Kiera Beitel does: "My mom says, 'Why do you have to have this shirt? What's wrong with that other one?' But if you don't have the right clothes and stuff, other kids make fun of you. If I wore the clothes my mom likes, I wouldn't even be able to go to school. It would be too embarrassing."

Your first few experiences with your kid's quest for the "right" stuff are not likely to be your last—in fact, with the teen years looming, this is probably just the beginning. But if you start to feel exasperated, try to remember how you felt about your looks and your peers—whether that look was overalls and a plaid shirt, the well-groomed "preppy" look, or something in between. Then you may realize just how crucial the right haircut can be.

WELCOME TO CYBERSPACE: KIDS ON THE NET

When 11-year-old Becca finally persuaded her mother to let her have a dog, she began researching breeds. They settled on a Brittany, and Cassie was soon a part of the family. There was only one problem, remembers Becca: "She wasn't so good with the old 'coming when you're called.'" Cassie's been improving lately, though, thanks to some training advice Becca got—on the Internet.

Becca, now 12, lives in New Zealand. So how do I know this story? Because our family has a Brittany pup, too, and we've become electronic pen pals through Becca's posting ("Anybody else got a Brittany?") on the "rec.dogs.behaviour" newsgroup.

This story illustrates both the wonderful and worrisome potential of kids exploring the info highway. The newsgroup Becca's been reading is, indeed, a source of good advice about dog training. It's also plagued by nasty infighting, "flaming" (a deluge of angry/insulting responses to a posting), and a dog-hater (or people-hater?) who periodically posts horrible replies to innocent questions ("You freaking idiot, I'll tell you how to stop that mutt's barking. Take a steel rod, and shove it down its...").

E-mail is another hornet's nest. My whole family has enjoyed reading Becca's letters, and there are Internet sites devoted to helping kids find "cyberpals" with shared interests or from other countries. What could be more fun and educational? But children also become vulnerable when they exchange e-mail addresses. Would you want your child to receive a message from Mr. Steel Rod?

The Internet is a new medium for families, and it has been heralded with genuine enthusiasm, plus some hype and alarm. If the educational value of the Net has been exaggerated, so have the dangers—yet both are real. So when the family goes on-line, parents need to think carefully

SAFETY NET FOR THE INTERNET
Basic ground rules for kids on the Net might start with:
- Don't give anyone personal information like your address, phone number, or school, or agree to meet anyone without your parents' permission.
- Don't buy or download anything without permission. (If your child will be downloading games, it's wise to have a virus-protection program on your computer.)
- Don't send nasty messages.
- "Walk away" from anything that makes you uncomfortable, whether it's ugly pictures on a Web site or a message that seems "off" on a chat line.

about how to help their kids enjoy the Net, and how to set safe and sensible limits.

"The Internet is so disorganized, so overwhelming, that people often wonder, 'Where do I start?'" notes Nyla Ahmad, editor-in-chief of *Owl* and *Chickadee* magazines for kids, and author of *CyberSurfer: The OWL Internet Guide for Kids*. "There's a huge amount of stuff out there, and much of it is not very useful or interesting. Kids usually start by looking for sites that relate to their interests, and that works well. They also look for things they're most familiar with: sports sites, sites for televisions shows, hobbies."

Deaglan Kernohan-Wallingford's family has been on-line for about a year now, and although his dad uses most of their monthly hours for his business, 11-year-old Deaglan is allowed to use any leftover time. How did he get started? "My dad showed me how to use the search engines on Netscape," says Deaglan, "and I just looked up things I'm interested in." He's demonstrating as we talk, taking me to one of his favourite sites, a George Lucas page with lots of *Star Wars* products and trivia. "They must have really updated this," he comments, scanning the screen for the link he wants, "because this is totally different from the last time I was here." As Deaglan tries out a couple of possibilities (both dead ends), I ask him whether he gets frustrated by the glitches and delays that seem to come with this new territory. He shrugs. "Sometimes graphics take a long time to load or something doesn't work. I don't really mind that much. I just try something else. It's still fun."

Ahmad acknowledges that right now, the Internet is more an entertainment medium than a source of education. "It is cumbersome to use as a conventional research tool. The Internet does not replace a library for doing your homework, although you can do a different kind of research, getting current information, even contacting the experts directly." Yet even if kids are just downloading games and reading baseball-player profiles, observes Ahmad, they are learning skills that will be valuable in the information age: "Children are growing up in a fingertip culture where they will need to be comfortable manipulating computer-generated material, and selecting from a vast and ever-changing body of information."

Ahmad notes that children are rarely intimidated by the maze-like, learn-as-you-go nature of the Net. Indeed, it's not unusual for older kids to be more confident—and competent—in cyberspace than their parents. But Ahmad urges parents to keep up, at least enough to be aware of what their child is doing. "In the beginning, I would say there should always be a parent there. The child is in the lead, making her own choices, but you're there to talk about what she finds to set limits and explain." With older, more experienced children, parents can just cruise by once in a while to glance at what's on the screen, and show their interest by asking how the session went. Still,

RECOMMENDED READING

CyberSurfer: The OWL Internet Guide for Kids, by Nyla Ahmad, OWL Books (Greey de Pencier), 1996. Includes a disk of "hot links" to sites of interest to kids.

Canadian Family On-Line: Every Parent's Guide to the Internet, by Wallace Whistance-Smith, Prentice-Hall, 1996.

Ahmad feels an adult should be present when kids are visiting news-groups or chat lines: "Children can tell the good stuff from the bad stuff, and they do learn what to steer clear of, but you have to help them with this," she stresses.

Ahmad's book (as well as the other title listed under "Recommended Reading," p. 111) provides a great array of Internet sites that are fun and safe for children. But even if your child never strays from these lists, you will still have to consider time limits. Long hours in front of the computer screen cut into time your child needs for creative play, exercise, reading, and homework. And unlike television, you pay for Internet use by the amount of time you spend on it—so whatever block of time you have purchased, you'll need some system to make sure that your kids share it fairly and don't exceed the monthly limit.

It's a brave new world all right, and it takes a little while to learn the ropes. But most families not only make peace with the Internet, they come to enjoy its many possibilities. So claim a little electronic highway time for yourself, too.

THE "JUNK" READING DEBATE:
EDIFYING—OR STUPEFYING?

committed my first and only act of public vandalism at the age of nine. The cause? Nancy Drew mysteries. My friend and I, newly converted to Nancy and having swapped the few volumes we had between us, had walked to our local library to check out some "further adventures." Not finding any in the stacks, I asked the librarian for help.

"We don't carry *those* books," she informed me haughtily. "They are simply junk!"

Well, I showed her. Meek and polite as ever, I settled myself into a desk in the corner...and proceeded to carve the words "Librarians are snotty!" into the varnished wood. I think I actually meant "snobby," but, hey, close enough.

Today, in my adult wisdom, I think "those books"—and their present-day counterparts (like the *Choose Your Own Adventure, Sweet Valley High, Babysitters' Club*, and, leading the pack, the *Goosebumps* and *Fear Street* series)—really are junk: repetitive, stereotypical, uninspired formula writing. But I also remember the sheer pleasure of whipping through one after another—and the outraged resentment I felt at that grown-up dismissal of my interest.

Why do kids like these books so much? And is there any harm in reading them?

"I think we have to concede that these books do have a role to play in children's reading development," says Phyllis Simon, a former children's librarian who owns Kidsbooks, a Vancouver bookstore. "Reading still isn't that easy for children at this age and, like a sport, the skills have to be consolidated with practice. The very predictability and lack of complexity we object to makes them easy to read, so kids can forget about the effort and just enjoy the story.

"I HATE READING"

Glen is a bright, happy ten-year-old. He does fairly well at school and has plenty of friends. He enjoys many sports and activities—but he doesn't enjoy reading. "It's boring," he says, shrugging. "I only read when I have to for school."

Glen *can* read—his skills are at the appropriate grade level. It's just that in his free time he prefers not to. Is this a problem?

It might be. Canadian author and educator Paul Kropp says that this is an age when some children fall seriously behind in their reading skills. "A kid who stops reading for himself develops reading abilities at half the rate of a kid who reads at home," says Kropp, author of *The Reading Solution* (Random House, 1993). "By high school his reading can be two grade levels behind. The mechanics of decoding letters is only the first stage of learning to read. To read longer, more challenging print, there's a whole new level of skill involved. And practice is essential to developing that skill."

"We can't force kids to enjoy reading," acknowledges Kropp, "but we can and should provide the opportunity and encouragement." His suggestions:

- Make time for reading. A daily half-hour "family reading time," when the TV is turned off and everyone reads *something*, underlines the value you place on reading. Reading can also happen at the traditional time—before bed. Consider condoning a later bedtime—*if* that time is spent reading in bed. "And if you've stopped reading to your child, pick it up again," says Kropp.
- Find the right stuff. To hook a reluctant reader on reading, you have to find the right hook. "Find out what their friends are reading," says Kropp. At this age, a friend's recommendation carries more weight than anything you or the librarian can give. Tap into his interests. There are books about nearly everything: horses, hockey, computers, rock bands. Magazines combine a specific interest with visual appeal and shorter, less overwhelming chunks of text—yet can still be a challenging read.
- Open your wallet. Yes, there's a library, but unenthusiastic readers tend to be unenthusiastic library-users. Ten bucks for the bookstore, on the other hand, may well get her browsing.

This can help them develop the fluency they need to move on to more challenging writing."

The problem, explains Simon, is that some kids never take that next step. "The children you worry about are the weaker readers who don't seem interested in widening their horizons, even after a year or two," says Simon. "There's a definite correlation in the later grades between how widely read a child is and his writing skills. Exposure to excellent writing strengthens children's grasp of vocabulary, sentence structure, narrative development. It's like the language seeps into them."

So if your preteen daughter checks out a stack of *Goosebumps* for the Christmas holidays, don't worry. She's discovered the pleasure of reading—and that's good. But also think about what you can do to introduce her to more inspired stuff.

Don't criticize. "We all read junk sometimes," says Simon. "Who are we to say kids aren't entitled to their own tastes and some down-time?" Besides, this is a tactic that can backfire badly. "You don't want me to read *The Saddle Club?* Fine, then I won't read anything at all!"

Keep reading aloud. Books that are too difficult for kids to read themselves are not necessarily beyond their understanding. This is where you come in. "If you've already been reading at bedtime or holiday afternoons, don't give up that tradition," advises Simon. "But don't read them the formula books that they can read on their own. Choose a great story you can both enjoy."

Gradually, says Simon, "the barriers between what they choose to read and the books you read together will break down, and they will start venturing out into more challenging material." It makes sense. Imagine getting really immersed in Madeleine L'Engle's *A Wrinkle in Time* or some Ray Bradbury sci-fi, and then returning to a *Choose Your Own Adventure* space story—it's bound to seem a bit flat by

EXPANDING THEIR HORIZONS

One great appeal of "series" books is that once a child finds something he likes, there's a raft of other titles he's also sure to enjoy. But after a while, that stream can run dry. "I'm tired of *Young Jedi Knights*, but I don't know what else to get." A children's librarian or bookseller can help by suggesting titles that have enough in common with your child's favourite series to be a good bet. Phyllis Simon, of Vancouver Kidsbooks, has some ideas to get you started.

IF YOUR CHILD LIKED:

- *The New Adventures of Mary-Kate and Ashley*, by I.K. Swobod, try: *Stella Street*, by Elizabeth Honey, *Bad Girls*, by Cynthia Voigt, *How Can I Be a Detective if I Have to Babysit?*, by Linda Bailey, or *Dimanch Diller*, by Henrietta Branford

- *The Saddle Club*, by Bonnie Bryant, try: *Horse Stories*, by Marguerite Henry, the *Black Stallion* series, by Walter Farley, or the *Animal Ark* series, by Lucy Daniels

- *Animorphs*, by K.A. Applegate, try: *Goblins in the Castle*, by Bruce Colville, the *Redwall* series, by Brian Jacques, or *Dial-a-Ghost*, by Eva Ibbotson

- *Survival!*, by K. Duey and K.A. Bale, try: *SOS Titanic*, by Eve Bunting, *Thunder Cave*, by Roland Smith, or *Far North*, by Will Hobbs

- *Star Wars: The Young Jedi Knights*, by Kevin J. Anderson and Rebecca Moesta, try: *The Castle in the Attic*, by Elizabeth Winthrop, *The Dragon-Slayers*, by K.H. McMullan, or *The Wizard of Earthsea*, by Ursula LeGuin

comparison. Maybe the better books are even worth the effort to read ahead without your dad.

Talk about the books you're reading. Preteens are interested in the adult world—including what adults read. So when your son says, "What's this book about?"—tell him, and tell him what you like about it. Better still, read one of the "good bits" aloud.

Some children—the voracious readers—will grow out of their "reading ruts" without your lifting a finger. But why leave it to luck, when there is such a pleasant way to exert a little parental influence? "Hopefully, teachers will continue to read aloud, too," adds Simon. "Really, kids never outgrow it."

THE JOY OF JUNK FOOD:
ENCOURAGING HEALTHY FOOD ATTITUDES

here was a time when you were in charge of every mouthful your child ate. You worried about starting solid foods at the right age, considered whether commercial baby foods were as nutritious as homemade ones, and read labels to make sure that there were no added sugars or chemicals.

But those days are long gone. Now your preteen trades his nutritious lunch for cream-filled cakes at school, picks up a chocolate bar on his way home, and cooks up frozen french fries in the toaster-oven for his after-school snack. Sometimes you think that "junk food" has become the mainstay of his diet. You can't go back to the days of spoon-feeding mixed vegetables, so how do you deal with the junk food problem?

The first step, says Michelle Hooper, nutrition programs officer with Health Canada, is to erase the words "junk food" from your vocabulary. "We're trying to get away from classifying foods as good foods and bad foods." Hooper recommends that parents promote the concepts of *Canada's Guide to Healthy Eating*, which stresses whole grains, fruits, vegetables, meats and other protein-rich foods and milk products, and also allows for "other foods," which can include some of those items we often call "junk."

Besides, bad-mouthing your child's favourite snack can make it even more tempting to his increasingly independent preteen sensibilities. If you disapprove, munching on potato chips becomes a great way to be defiant (and they taste pretty good, too!).

Jody Davis discovered that restricting these treats too firmly can lead to greater problems. "When my daughter Grace was younger, we didn't allow any sweets or junk food in the house, so she didn't even know about them. That all changed once she started school, and we

THE FACTS ABOUT DIETARY FAT

Dietary fat and cholesterol are in the news a lot these days—but it's a complex issue that leaves many of us slightly bemused. And when it comes to our kids, we may have even more questions. What *should* we do about the level of fat in our kids' diet?

Louise Lambert-Lagacé, a Montreal consulting dietitian and co-author of *Good Fat, Bad Fat* (Stoddart, 1995), has sensible and encouraging advice for confused parents. "Unless there's a strong family history of health problems related to dietary fat and cholesterol, we shouldn't be worrying about our children's fat intake," says Lambert-Lagacé. "We *do*, of course, want to be encouraging a healthy diet—and would ideally like to see fat contributing 30 percent or less of the total diet by the teen years. But there are better, more positive ways to do that than restricting food or trying to 'scare' kids away from fat."

So what can parents do? Concentrate, advises Lambert-Lagacé, on *adding* into the family diet those foods that Canadians tend to eat too little of: fresh fruit and vegetables, whole grains, fish. As Lambert-Lagacé points out, "By encouraging these 'neglected' foods, we automatically lower our intake of some of the other high-fat foods that we may be over-emphasizing."

Some specific ideas:

- Prepare "good-fat" foods with an appealing twist: barbecue salmon steaks, set up a create-your-own-salad bar, offer trail mix (a combination of nuts and dried fruit) as a fast snack.
- Do go easy on the fried foods. Light sautéing is better than deep-fat frying; better still is using oil to flavour food *after* it is cooked, for example, brushing cooked potatoes with olive oil and lemon juice.
- Try a few simple switches in your grocery basics: use canola or olive oil for salad dressing and cooking; romaine instead of iceberg lettuce; whole-grain instead of white bread and rice.
- Take advantage of your preteen's increased openness to new foods to introduce a new (healthy) dish or two. Visit ethnic restaurants whose cuisine is less "red-meat heavy" than ours; maybe Thai noodles or tabouli will become a new favourite!

had some huge battles because she wanted the Twinkies and things that other kids were eating. She'd trade what I sent her for lunch for the other kids' snacks—she'd even offer to do their homework to get a treat."

Davis thought her nutrition messages had finally got through when Grace stopped eating the offending foods at around age 11, but she soon discovered her daughter had actually become anorexic. "We've been going through a lot of treatment and I know it isn't the only issue, but now I wish I hadn't tried to control her eating so much. It became a battleground between the two of us, and that's not healthy."

A 1996 Health Canada report, *Food for Thought*, described the results of focus-group meetings with both children and parents to discuss nutrition. They found that the kids aged ten to twelve described foods such as candy, chips, and soft drinks as "bad," yet still consumed more of these than their parents found acceptable. The children also mentioned that one of their reasons for choosing these foods was that they were instant snacks.

Hooper reminds parents that kids are not the same as adults, and their nutritional needs are different. Children in this age group, she points out, are on the verge of puberty. "Kids grow at different rates," Hooper explains, "but just before puberty begins most kids will gain some weight in preparation for that rapid growth spurt. And preteens who are growing rapidly will be hungry most of the time."

Parents who have become accustomed to the slower growth rate of younger children sometimes are amazed by the voracious appetites of preteens and adolescents. "A growing child who is active—perhaps involved in sports or other high-energy activities—may find it very hard to get enough calories without eating some of the higher-fat foods that we consider junk foods," Hooper says.

The National Institute of Nutrition's Fall 1995 *Healthy Bites* publication includes some great suggestions for easy snacks. Try to find out what your child feels like eating:

Something crunchy? Offer an apple, celery sticks with peanut butter, dry breakfast cereal, carrot and green pepper strips with dip.

Something thirst-quenching? Offer a yogurt drink, a fruit-juice popsicle, an orange, or a slice of watermelon.

Something hearty and filling? How about leftover pizza, fig bars, cheese and crackers, or dried fruit and nuts mixed together?

Something sweet? Whole-grain toast with honey or a cinnamon-sugar mixture, or perhaps a baked apple drizzled with a little maple syrup.

Stocking up the fridge and cupboards with nutritious snacks that pre-teens can easily serve themselves encourages them to eat a wider variety: fresh fruits and prepared veggies, trail mix, whole-grain muffins, yogurt...And guess what popular, easily prepared food fits the bill nicely? Breakfast cereal—it's a good source of grains and contains added iron.

Hooper also makes the point that "treat" foods are often an important part of social activities. "If your child is invited to a birthday party or gets together with friends after school, they're going to eat ice cream and potato chips and drink pop. And your child should be able to enjoy those foods and the time with his friends, without feeling guilty that he's eating 'bad' foods."

THE SPORTING LIFE: SUPPORTING YOUNG ATHLETES

hen Ariel Elliott was seven years old, her family went on vacation to Prince Edward Island. There she had her first ride on a pony and, according to her mother, Kim, "That was it." From that moment on, horses and riding became Ariel's passion.

Now she's 11, and spends as much time as she can with horses: lessons twice a week, plus visits to the barn to clean stalls, groom horses, and watch other classes as often as she can persuade her parents (or anyone else!) to take her. During show season, she's even busier, with at least one weekend each month taken up by a show.

Not that Ariel minds. "She'd be at the barn all the time if I let her," says Kim.

Many children enjoy sports, but for most of them athletics is a "sideline" in their life—a fun activity, not the dominant theme. Being heavily involved in a sport, though—whether it's riding, gymnastics, or hockey—requires a huge investment in time and energy, not only on the part of the young participant but from the parents, too. The Elliotts, for example, spend many hours driving Ariel to and from the riding stable and watching her ride at shows (her mother also volunteers at the shows). Cost is another issue—and horseback riding is one of the more expensive activities, especially when the junior rider is competing.

Hockey is another sport that can require incredible levels of commitment from the athlete's entire family. Zachary Katsof, now 15, has been playing hockey since he was six. At ten, he made the "Rep" team and began competing across the region, instead of just locally. "It was hard to adjust at first," he says. "Sometimes we had two- or three-hour bus trips to get to games, and I had to make myself do my homework on the bus or I wouldn't have time after."

OTHER PASSIONS

It isn't always a sports activity that soaks up large amounts of a preteen's time, energy, and enthusiasm. Catherine, aged 12, is dedicated to ballet and takes eight classes a week—plus additional rehearsal time when she's preparing for a performance. "I know that even professional dancers have to keep on taking lessons all the time," Catherine says. "This is the only way to be good at ballet, doing it every day. Once a week just won't work."

Acting is another activity that can become a way of life, especially if it develops into a career. Lisa began acting in commercials when she was seven; by the time she was nine she'd had several small parts in made-for-TV movies and some Canadian shows. At 11, she flew out to California for the first time to act in a network TV show, and her success there led to several other parts.

Although she had a tutor while she was filming on location, Lisa found that she wasn't always in step with her classmates, and she missed the opportunities to work with school friends on projects. Because her schedule was less predictable than that of kids taking lessons or competing in a team sport, she found it hard to be involved in any other activities. At any time a call from her agent could mean a quickly arranged trip to a new location.

For Lisa, those things were less important than the opportunity to do something she loves to do. (Her whole family eventually moved to California, reducing travel time and allowing her to attend school with other young actors.)

If your child becomes passionately committed to any activity, your ongoing support will be critical. You will have to make difficult decisions at times. How much time and money can you afford to invest in this? Can you keep your child's life in some kind of balance when a single activity seems to dominate? How does this affect other members of the family? Your child will see only his goal. Your role, as a parent, is to keep in mind the bigger picture, with everyone's well-being in mind.

Zachary's mother, Janice, adds, "The investment is unbelievable, between the money and the time. I have to confess that we didn't know much about hockey before Zach got interested in it, and we had no idea what it was going to cost."

Since the age of ten, Zachary has played hockey four or five times a week: usually three practices and two games. Each game or practice takes up two and a half hours—longer when you add transportation time for out-of-town games. Often weekends are completely consumed by tournaments.

The Katsofs try to attend all of their son's games, but if they go together, they have to bring along Zachary's two younger sisters. "A lot of the time that's a problem," says Janice, "because the arenas are unheated and they get cold and bored just sitting there. But I don't want them to go off into the heated area where I can't keep an eye on them." She adds that for many parents, hockey becomes their whole social life; there isn't much time for anything else.

Like many determined athletes, both Ariel and Zach have maintained good grades in school and manage to participate in other activities. Zachary plays soccer during the summer, has appeared in school plays, and is active in his synagogue's youth group. Kim, commenting on her daughter's non-riding achievements, says: "It's all part and parcel of the same thing. The exercise she gets from riding and the skills she develops in controlling the horse and mastering the show requirements keep her fit physically and sharp mentally. I think her involvement in riding helps her do better in school."

It may well. Research on children and sports tends to support Kim's feelings that this is beneficial to Ariel's life. Michelle Brownrigg, research co-ordinator at the Ontario Physical and Health Education Association, says, "The obvious benefits are physical, but sports can contribute to the child's mental, emotional, and social development as well." Sports can help children develop self-esteem and confidence as they learn and perform new skills; they can also learn persistence, problem-solving, and strategies to cope with stress and pressure.

Brownrigg adds, "Children who are very involved in a sport learn time management skills and how to set priorities. Being fit and active also gives them the extra energy needed to be involved in many things."

Is there a downside? Certainly, kids who take on a heavy training and competing schedule are at risk of "burn-out"—too much pressure, too many demands to juggle, too little time to just relax and be a kid. Parents have to keep an eye on the emotional well-being of their budding athletes, and help them find an appropriate balance.

Brownrigg stresses that in order for sports to be a positive experience for children, it has to remain fun. "Kids take part in sports because they want to have fun, learn new things, and be active with other kids," she explains. If they aren't having fun, or if the activity becomes boring because there are no new challenges, children can be turned off sports altogether.

"An overemphasis on winning can take all the fun out of sports as well," Brownrigg adds. "Parents and coaches should put value on the process as well as the outcome. That means talking about what the child enjoyed, about new things the child tried or accomplished, and not just focusing on whether they won or lost."

The benefits of sports are still there when children play at lower intensities, Brownrigg says. "They still have the opportunity to enjoy being active, to learn physical skills, to have fun playing, and to interact with other kids as teammates or opponents. These are valuable lessons for any child."

KIDS WITH A CAUSE: THE YOUNG CRUSADER

. . . .

Your ten-year-old daughter has become your very own home version of the "Environment Police." She scorns the disposable sandwich bags you used to put her lunch in and insists on having reusable containers—something you've avoided in the past because they always get deformed in the dishwasher. She protests the existence of every cleaning product and spray can in the house. Now she has taken to fishing through the garbage in case you've tossed out something that could have been recycled...and it's driving you crazy.

This desire to take a stand is not unusual for preteens and teenagers. Jacqui Barnes, a director at Animal Alliance in Toronto, says that many young people between the ages of nine and fifteen contact her organization for information about animal rights. "This is an age of growing awareness about issues, about ethics, about the environment and the world around them," she observes.

Barnes says the dawning commitment to a cause often begins with a school project or assignment. "As students begin to research topics, their eyes are opened. We get a lot of calls about the use of animals in cosmetics testing, for example. Kids call the cosmetics companies and find out that it's hard to get information, so they come to us." Often, she says, they are surprised to learn about the tests that are done and what happens to the animals.

"Young children are naturally compassionate, and their concern for others—humans and animals—isn't yet blunted by practical concerns," Barnes adds.

The interest in animal rights among young people has been so high that Animal Alliance has created a Web site for kids as an adjunct to their adult Web site (www.animalalliance.ca). "Kids who are interested in causes often get brushed off by adults," Barnes says. "People think it's just a fad or a phase that they'll grow out of soon." Barnes doesn't see it that way. She believes these young people are educating themselves about critical issues and developing their own opinions as a result.

Many put that commitment to a cause into action. Noah Stewart-Ornstein, for example, who has just turned 12, has already done presentations to other students about animal rights and vegetarianism. He says, "I did a debate at school in front of an audience, and the vegetarian side—my side—won. I just feel it's wrong to kill animals and eat them when it's unnecessary. Some people don't want to think about these issues, but I think they're important."

Noah has convinced his entire family to become vegetarian ("although my dad still eats meat sometimes"), and says he's won a number of other people over to his cause. "The cafeteria at our school was cooking french fries in the same oil as the meat, so I got a campaign to stop that, too." While his school debates and presentations have been effective, Noah feels his informal conversations with others have also been an important way to spread the message.

David Wyatt, the head of the science department at Grimsby Secondary School in Grimsby, Ontario, says that many elementary school students continue their interest in issues such as the environment when they enter high school. He is the teacher responsible for SCAPE (Students Concerned about Planet Earth), a school club that gives students a chance to take on a number of environmental issues. "We tackle both local projects—cleaning up Forty Mile Creek here in Grimsby and setting up a recycling and composting program in the school, for example—and global projects, such as fund-raising for Greenpeace and the rainforest," explains Wyatt.

Wyatt adds, "These young people have a really deep-seated caring for the environment and are looking for a vehicle to do something to help out, to make a difference." He notes that it can be frustrating for the

GIVING TO OTHERS

Despite book titles like *Looking Out for Number One* and T-shirts that announce "Winning is everything," altruism is still alive and well among preteens and teens. There are many kids who are contributing to their communities in small but important ways. Consider these examples:

- Three brothers, ranging in age from ten to eighteen, create a not-too-scary "haunted house" for children in foster care, and escort the children through on Halloween.
- Grade-six students at a public school organize a skip-a-thon and raise more than $2000 to help needy children.
- Preteens volunteer in the church nursery during services, helping to cuddle the babies and play with the toddlers.

Encouraging children to give of themselves is a valuable lesson, both for the help it provides to others, and for the good feeling it grants the giver. But "the goal is for the children to do things for others of their own volition, not because someone tells them to or because they are forced to," says Julie Hayes, a child and youth counsellor who works with disadvantaged children in Burlington, Ontario. "Parents should not look for instant results or expect too much," adds Hayes. "A child may need to take from you for a long time before he feels ready to give to someone else."

Carol Gallant, the mother of two teenage daughters, remembers that the first time she took her daughters and some of their friends to help out at the food bank, most of the young people (all in their early teens) just stood around and talked. "Only two out of the seven really did anything helpful," she says. But a week later, all seven teens received thank-you cards from the food bank staff, and that made them eager to go back again. "Now all seven are active volunteers."

Hayes says that parents need to model the idea of giving to others for their children. "We're all so busy that it's hard to find time to do volunteer work, and nobody ever feels they have enough money to make a charitable donation. But if these are values we want our children to learn, it's important to demonstrate them in action."

She encourages parents to find ways of helping that they can manage. Some volunteer tasks need only an hour or so a week; other agencies just need people to help with special events once or twice a year. Finally, Hayes stresses the idea of community. "Helping others doesn't have to be part of a formal program with volunteer training. We are all part of a community, we're all in this together. You could help out by offering to babysit for the single parent living on your street or by taking a meal to a neighbour who is ill." Kids can follow suit by walking the neighbour's child to school, or raking leaves for a grandparent.

Children who learn to contribute to the wider community will quickly reap rich rewards, according to Hayes. "When young people help others their own problems seem smaller and they realize that they're not the only ones who have problems. They feel more powerful, too—after all, they were able to help somebody, so they must be capable."

younger child, who is concerned about issues but can't yet participate in these groups.

Noah agrees. "People think it's just a fad, or that I'm just trying to be different. It's hard to get taken seriously at my age. But this is something I really believe is important."

It's easy for cynical adults to feel some amusement when idealistic preteens become young zealots, or to feel irritated when their commitment to some cause makes our own lives more difficult. But children in this age group can and do make a difference. Think of Craig Kielburger, the 12-year-old Toronto boy who was horrified when he read about the child labour problem around the world. He became a highly effective advocate for this cause, speaking at conferences around the world. At age 13 he founded "Free the Children," an organization for young people aged 8 to 18 who are concerned about child labour. It was Craig who persuaded Prime Minister Jean Chrétien to make child labour an issue for Canada in dealing with other countries.

Few children will achieve international fame because of their support of a cause, but they all deserve our respect. There's a lot of work needed to make the world a better place—and every little bit helps.

Recommended Reading

Your favourite parenting books will still be useful, but more and more you'll find you're looking for approaches that are particularly helpful with older kids. Take a look at:

Discipline that Works: Promoting Self-Discipline in Children, by Dr. Thomas Gordon, Plume Books, 1989.

The Hurried Child: Growing Up Too Fast, Too Soon, by David Elkind, Addison-Wesley, 1988.

The Portable Pediatrician's Guide to Kids: Your Child's Physical and Behavioral Development from Ages 5 to 12, by Laura Walther Nathanson, MD, FAAP, HarperPerennial, 1996.

The Roller-Coaster Years: Raising Your Child through the Maddening Yet Magical Middle School Years, by Charlene C. Giannetti and Margaret Sagarese, Broadway Books, 1997.

And, for a sneak preview on parenting teenagers, here's a book that combines humour and great advice:

Get Out of My Life, But First Could You Drive Me and Cheryl to the Mall? A Parent's Guide to the New Teenager, by Anthony E. Wolf, Noonday Press, 1991.